American English in Mind

Herbert Puchta & Jeff Stranks

Student's Book Starter

CAMBRIDGE
UNIVERSITY PRESS

CAMBRIDGE UNIVERSITY PRESS
Cambridge, New York, Melbourne, Madrid, Cape Town, Singapore,
São Paulo, Delhi, Dubai, Tokyo, Mexico City

Cambridge University Press
32 Avenue of the Americas, New York, NY 10013-2473, USA

www.cambridge.org
Information on this title: www.cambridge.org/9780521733236

First published 2011

Printed in Hong Kong, China, by Sheck Wah Tong Printing Press Limited

A catalog record for this publication is available from the British Library.

ISBN 978-0-521-73323-6 Student's Book Starter
ISBN 978-0-521-73324-3 Starter Combo A
ISBN 978-0-521-73325-0 Starter Combo B
ISBN 978-0-521-73329-8 Workbook Starter
ISBN 978-0-521-73330-4 Teacher's Edition Starter
ISBN 978-0-521-73331-1 Class Audio Starter
ISBN 978-0-521-73326-7 Classware Starter
ISBN 978-0-521-73332-8 Testmaker Starter
ISBN 978-0-521-73343-4 DVD Starter

Art direction, book design and layout: Pentacor plc
Photo research: Pronk and Associates

Contents

Unit	Grammar	Vocabulary	Pronunciation
1 The world around me	Regular plural nouns, irregular plural nouns	The day, international words, classroom objects	Syllables
2 Do you understand?	Adjectives, *a/an*	The alphabet, colors, numbers 1–100 Everyday English	Letter sounds
CHECK YOUR PROGRESS			
3 He's a soccer player.	The verb *be* (singular): statements and questions Question words: *Who, What, How old, Where?*	Countries and nationalities	*from*
4 We're a new band.	The verb *be* (plural): negatives and questions *I (don't) like … / Do you like …?* Object pronouns	Affirmative and negative adjectives Everyday English	/ɪ/ and /i/
CHECK YOUR PROGRESS			
5 She lives in Washington.	Simple present: affirmative and negative; questions and short answers Possessive *'s*; possessive adjectives	Family	/s/, /z/ and /ɪz/
6 Where's the market?	*there's / there are* Affirmative imperatives Prepositions of place	Places in towns, numbers 100+ Everyday English	/ð/ and /θ/
CHECK YOUR PROGRESS			
7 They have brown eyes.	*has/have* *Why …? Because …*	Parts of the body	/v/ *have*
8 This is delicious!	*I'd like / Would you like …?* Count and noncount nouns *this/that/these/those*	Food Everyday English	/w/ *would*
CHECK YOUR PROGRESS			
9 I sometimes watch TV.	Simple present with adverbs of frequency	Days of the week, TV shows, telling the time	Compound nouns
10 Don't do that!	Negative imperatives	Adjectives to describe feelings Everyday English	Linking sounds
CHECK YOUR PROGRESS			
11 Yes, I can!	*can/can't* (ability) *like / don't like + -ing*	Sports	*can/can't*
12 A bad storm's coming.	Present continuous	House and furniture Everyday English	/h/ *have*
CHECK YOUR PROGRESS			
13 Special days	*can/can't* (asking for permission) Prepositions: *at, in, on* *one/ones*	Months of the year and seasons, clothes	/æ/ and /e/
14 He was only 22.	Simple past: *was/wasn't; were/weren't*	Time expressions, ordinal numbers and dates Everyday English	*was/wasn't* and *were/weren't*
CHECK YOUR PROGRESS			
15 What happened?	Simple past: regular and irregular verbs; questions and negatives	Verb and noun pairs	*-ed* endings
16 Things change.	Comparative adjectives *than*	Adjectives and opposites Everyday English	*than*
CHECK YOUR PROGRESS			

Speaking & Functions	Listening	Reading	Writing
Saying *hello* and *goodbye* Asking and answering what something is in English	Dialogues practicing *hello* and *goodbye*	Dialogues: Saying *hello* and *goodbye* Culture in mind: Different ways to say *hello*	Conversation between old and new friends
Asking and answering Saying how many people and things there are Last but not least: taking down / leaving phone messages	Article about being polite	Article: Being polite Photostory: Is this your hat?	Phone message
Saying where you and other people are from Talking about heroes	Dialogues about celebrities and heroes	Dialogue: Waiting in line Culture in mind: Heroes	Short description about yourself
Talking about: likes and dislikes; celebrities you like or don't like Last but not least: asking a celebrity questions	Interview with a new band Conversation about celebrities Song: "Are We Alone?"	Interview: A new band Photostory: Just a little joke	Email about your favorite band
Talking about: the present; your family	Dialogue about free-time activities	Article: America's First Lady Culture in mind: American families	Paragraph about your family
Talking about places in a town Last but not least: giving directions to tourists	Dialogue about asking for and giving directions	Wegpage: Things to see and do in Boston Dialogue: Directions Photostory: A charity run	Short text about your town or city
Asking and answering questions with *have* Describing people Giving personal information	Descriptions of people	Article: Sally or Paula? Culture in mind: Different cultures – different pets	Two short descriptions of friends or family members
Ordering food in a restaurant Last but not least: talking about food you like and dislike	Dialogue in a restaurant	Article: Unusual food around the world Photostory: Enjoy your lunch!	Email about likes and dislikes
Talking about: routines; TV shows	Dialogues about TV likes, dislikes and habits	Article: Different places – different lives Culture in mind: What American teenagers watch	Paragraph about TV shows you like
Talking about how you feel Last but not least: playing a game of Simon Says	A picture story Song: "Don't Stop"	Email about feelings Photostory: Kate looks great!	Email to an old friend
Talking about: abilities; likes and dislikes	Amazing abilities Conversation about sports	Article: We never win, but we always win Culture in mind: Not only baseball, basketball and football	Email about sports
Describing what is happening now Talking about your house or apartment Last but not least: talking about a vacation	A telephone conversation about what is happening now Sounds of everyday activities	Article: Around the world – alone Photostory: Just five minutes!	A vacation postcard
Talking about: times and dates; what someone is wearing; clothes and shopping	Description of models in a fashion show	Article: Scotland – a land of traditions Culture in mind: The Edinburgh Festival	Email about a special festival in your country
Talking about the past Last but not least: talking about when you were very young	Conversation about the Beatles	Article: The history of pop Text: A rooftop concert Photostory: An accident in the park	Email to a friend about a vacation
Asking and answering questions in a questionnaire	Radio quiz show about historic events	Article: She said "no" Culture in mind: The mother of TV	Paragraph about a famous person from the past
Comparing people and things in the classroom Describing things using adjectives Comparing things Last but not least: giving a presentation comparing past and present in your country	Conversation comparing the 1960s with the present	Article: From London bank to Thailand hotel Photostory: So sorry.	Competition entry comparing life in the past and present

1 The world around me

* Saying *hello* and *goodbye*
* Regular plural nouns, irregular plural nouns
* Vocabulary: the day, international words, classroom objects

1 Read and listen

* Saying *hello* and *goodbye*

a Look at the pictures. What are the people doing? Read the dialogues quickly to check your ideas.

b ▶ **CD1 T02** Now read the dialogues again and listen. Then practice the dialogues with a partner.

Paula: Hey, Steve. How are you?
Steve: Fine, thanks. And you?
Paula: I'm OK.

Joanne: Hello, Mrs. Jackson.
Mrs. Jackson: Hi, Joanne. How are you?
Joanne: I'm fine, thank you. Well, goodbye.
Mrs. Jackson: Goodbye.

Sandra: Bye, Mike.
Mike: Bye, Sandra. See you later.
Sandra: Yeah, see you.

c Read the dialogues again. Write the words in the table.

~~hello~~ hey goodbye hi
see you later bye

Saying *hello*	Saying *goodbye*
hello	

② Vocabulary

✱ The day

a Match the words with the pictures.

morning   afternoon   ~~evening~~   night

1 .... *evening*

2 ....

3 ....

4 ....

b ▶ **CD1 T03** What are the people saying? Write the numbers in the speech bubbles. Then listen and check.

1 Good morning.

2 Good afternoon.

3 Good evening.

4 Good night.

5 Goodbye.

✳ International words

C ▶ CD1 T04 Write the words from the box under the pictures. Then listen, check and repeat.

airport bus café ~~city~~ DVD hamburger hotel museum TV
phone pizza restaurant sandwich taxi computer music

1 _____city_____

2 _____

3 _____

4 _____

5 _____

6 _____

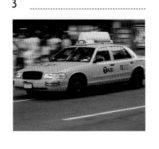

7 _____

8 _____

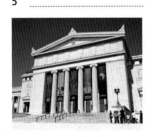

9 _____

10 _____

11 _____

12 _____

13 _____

14 _____

15 _____

16 _____

d Work with a partner. Say a name you know for each place.

A: *a restaurant*
B: *Tina's Tacos*

1 a restaurant
2 a city
3 a museum
4 a television show
5 a café
6 a hotel

3 Speak

✱ Classroom objects

a Work with a partner. What are these things in English? Write the words under the pictures.

notebook   book   CD   pencil   ~~pen~~   desk   board   window   door   chair

1 _____pen_____   2 _____   3 _____   4 _____   5 _____

6 _____   7 _____   8 _____   9 _____   10 _____

b ▶ CD1 T05   Listen and check your answers.

c Work with a partner. Ask and answer questions about the pictures.

A: *What's picture 1 in English?*
B: *It's a pen.*

4 Grammar

✱ Regular plural nouns

a Look at the examples. Complete the rule.

hotel   hotels   TV   TVs
taxi   taxis   bus   bus**es**

> **RULE:** For most words, add _____ to make the plural. For words that end in _____ , z, ch, sh, or x, add -es to make the plural.

b Write the words under the pictures.

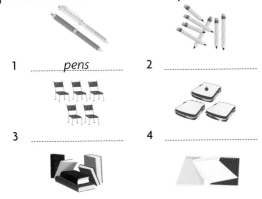

1 _____pens_____   2 _____

3 _____   4 _____

5 _____   6 _____

✱ Irregular plural nouns

c Match the singular and plural nouns.

Singular	Plural
1 one man	a eight people
2 one woman	b two men
3 one person	c three children
4 one child	d three women

5 Pronunciation

▶ CD1 T06 and 07   Pronunciation section starts on page 114.

Culture in mind

6 Read and listen

a ▶ CD1 T08 Read about greetings. What's a short way to write *How are you?*

b Check the greetings without words.

1 a hug ☐
2 hello ☐
3 a bow ☐
4 hey ☐
5 a wave ☐
6 a handshake ☐

c Think of three ways to greet people in your own language.

d Share your ideas with a partner.

Different ways to say

Greetings without words

a wave

a bow

7 Write

a Complete the conversation with the words in the box.

hey   thanks   how   up   OK

Diane: _____ , Eddie.

Eddie: Hi, Diane. _____ are you?

Diane: I'm fine, _____ . And you?

Eddie: I'm _____ . This is my friend, Eva.

Diane: Hi, Eva. What's _____ ?

Eva: Not much. Nice to meet you.

Informal

What's up?

How are you?

a handshake

a high five

a hug

b Write a conversation between you, a friend and a new friend.

You: Hey, _____ .

Your friend: _____ , _____ .
_____ ?

You: I'm _____ , thanks. _____ ?

Your friend: I'm _____ . This is my friend, _____ .

You: Hi, _____ . _____ ?

New friend: Not much. _____ .

8 Speak

a Work in groups of three. Act out your conversations from Exercise 7b.

b Act out the conversations again. Include greetings without words (a wave, a bow, a handshake or a high five).

2 **Do you understand?**

* Asking and answering
* Adjectives, *a/an*
* Vocabulary: the alphabet, colors, numbers 0–100

1 **Read and listen**

* Asking and answering

a Read the article quickly. What is it about?

> # Being polite
>
> There are many things you can say to be polite. Look at these tips.
>
> - You don't understand something. Ask, "What does this mean?" Or say, "I don't understand."
>
> - You want someone's attention. Say, "Excuse me ... "
>
> - You need help. Ask, "Can you help me?"
>
> - Someone asks you a question. Tell them the answer. If you don't know the answer, say, "I'm sorry. I don't know."
>
> - Someone needs help. Ask, "Can I help you?" Or say, "I can help you."
>
> > **Other polite phrases:**
> > - Please.
> > - Thank you.
> > - You're welcome.
> > - No problem.

b ▶ **CD1 T09** Now read the article again and listen. Then complete the conversations with words from Exercise 1a.

Daniel: I don't ___understand___ this problem.
Marcos: I can _____ _____ .

Emily: What does this _____ ?
Ahmed: I'm _____ . I _____ know.

Beverly: _____ me ... Can you
_____ _____ , please?
Cassandra: Sure. No _____ .
Beverly: _____ you.
Cassandra: You're _____ .

Jackie: _____ I _____ you?
Ted: Yes, please. Where's Main Street?

c Work with a partner. Practice the conversations from Exercise 1b.

2 Grammar

✻ Adjectives

a Write the phrases from the box under the pictures.

> a big TV   an old desk   a new book   a small hotel   a bad café
> an interesting museum   ~~a cheap computer~~   a good hamburger

1 _a cheap computer_   2 _____   3 _____   4 _____

5 _____   6 _____   7 _____   8 _____

b ▶ CD1 T10   Listen, check and repeat.

c Put the words in the correct order.

1 city / big / a   _a big city_
2 DVD / good /a   _____
3 restaurant / an / expensive   _____
4 interesting / book / an   _____
5 soccer team / good / a   _____
6 computer game / an / interesting _____

d Work with a partner. Give examples from Exercise 2c.

A: *a big city*
B: *Tokyo*

e Match the opposites.

1 good   _c_   a interesting
2 big   _____   b new
3 boring   _____   c bad
4 old   _____   d small
5 cheap   _____   e expensive

✻ *a/an*

f Look at the examples. Complete the rule.

*a **b**ig restaurant*
*a **g**ood teacher*
*an **e**xpensive hotel*
*an **i**nteresting movie*

> **RULE:** We use _____ before words beginning with a consonant (*b, c, d, f,* etc.), and we use _____ before words beginning with a vowel (*a, e, i, o, u*).

g Write *a* or *an*.

1 _a_ good book
2 _____ old chair
3 _____ expensive computer
4 _____ big taxi
5 _____ small pizza
6 _____ international airport

3 Vocabulary

* The alphabet

a ▶ CD1 T11 Listen to the alphabet. Then listen again and repeat.

A a	J j	S s
B b	K k	T t
C c	L l	U u
D d	M m	V v
E e	N n	W w
F f	O o	X x
G g	P p	Y y
H h	Q q	Z z
I i	R r	

b Write the missing letters.

1 C   *D*   E   F   ....
2 M   N   ....   P   ....
3 ....   S   ....   U   V
4 A   ....   D   E
5 J   L   ....   N
6 ....   W   X   ....   Z

c Work with a partner. Spell the names of the people.

R-I-H-A-N-N-A

1 a famous person
2 your teacher
3 your parents
4 a friend

4 Pronunciation

▶ CD1 T12 Pronunciation section starts on page 114.

5 Vocabulary

* Colors

a Write the colors under the soccer shirts.

silver   black   blue   brown   green
gray   orange   pink   purple   red
yellow   ~~white~~

1 .... *white* ....   2 ....

3 ....   4 ....

5 ....   6 ....

7 ....   8 ....

9 ....   10 ....

11 ....   12 ....

b ▶ CD1 T13 Listen and check.

c Find things in your classroom and say the colors.

a red pen
brown chairs

6 Vocabulary

❋ Numbers 0–20

a ▶ **CD1 T14** Write the missing numbers. Then listen, check and repeat.

0	zero / "oh"	7	seven	14	fourteen
1	one	....	eight	....	fifteen
2	two	9	nine	16	sixteen
_3_	three	10	ten	....	seventeen
4	four	11	eleven	18	eighteen
....	five	....	twelve	19	nineteen
6	six	13	thirteen	20	twenty

b Complete the conversations with the words for the numbers.

A: What's your phone number?

B: It's ____two____ , _____ ,
   _____ – ____four____ ,
   _____ , _____ ,
   _____

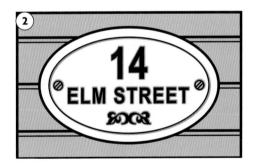

A: What's your address?

B: It's _____ Elm Street.

A: What's your favorite number?

B: _____ .

c Practice the conversations from Exercise 6b with a partner. Then practice the conversations with your own information. Make up numbers if you don't want to give your own.

❋ Numbers 20–100

d ▶ **CD1 T15** Listen and repeat the numbers.

20	twenty	70	seventy
30	thirty	80	eighty
40	forty	90	ninety
50	fifty	100	one hundred / a hundred
60	sixty		

e ▶ **CD1 T16** (Circle) and then write the number you hear.

1 10 /(20)   ____twenty____
2 30 / 40   _____
3 19 / 90   _____
4 40 / 50   _____
5 60 / 70   _____
6 18 / 80   _____

7 Speak

❋ Numbers 0–100

Work with a partner. Say the numbers.

1 people in your class
2 teachers in your school
3 books in your class
4 pens on your desk

Is this your hat?

8 Read and listen

a ▶ **CD1 T17** Look at the photostory. Who finds a hat? Whose hat is it? Read and listen to find the answer.

1

Kate: What's this? Oh! A hat!

2

Jo: Hi, Mark. Can you answer my phone?
Mark: Sure, Jo.

3

Mark: Hello? Meadow Hall.
Izzie: Hello. May I speak to Jo?
Mark: Sorry, Jo's busy. Can I take a message?
Izzie: Yes, this is Izzie.
Mark: *Iz-* What? How do you spell your name?
Izzie: It's Isabella. But call me Izzie, I-Z-Z-I-E.
Mark: OK, Izzie. What's your phone number?
Izzie: It's two-one-two, six-four-nine, five-nine-six-zero.
Mark: OK. Thanks, Izzie. Bye.
Izzie: Goodbye.

4

Jo: Darren, can you help me?
Darren: Sure. No problem, Jo.
Jo: Thanks.

5

Kate: Whose hat is this?
Darren: I don't know. Mark?
Mark: It's not mine.
Jo: It's my hat. Thanks, Kate!

b Mark the statements *T* (true) or *F* (false).

1 Mark answers the phone. ☐
2 Jo is busy. ☐
3 Isabella's nickname is Issa. ☐
4 Isabella's phone number is 212-659-4960. ☐

9 Everyday English

a Find the expressions in the photostory. Who says them?

1 What's this? _____Kate_____
2 busy _____
3 What? _____
4 call me _____

b How do you say each of the expressions in Exercise 9a in your language?

c ▶ CD1 T18 Read the dialogue and put the sentences in the correct order. Then listen and check.

☐ Deidra: Deidra. D-E-I-D-R-A. But you can call me Dee.

☐ Jill: *De-* What?

☐1 Jill: Hello?

☐ Deidra: Hi. May I speak to Tom?

☐ Deidra: Sure. This is Deidra.

☐ Jill: I'm sorry, he's busy. Can I take a message?

(Later)

☐8 Jill: Oh, it's a message from Dee.

☐ Tom: Hey, what's this?

d Underline the correct option.

1
A: Hi, Jennifer.
B: *Call me / What* Jenny.

2
A: What's *this / it's*?
B: It's a notebook.

3
A: Can I talk to Tom?
B: I'm sorry. He's *not / busy*.

4
A: Hi. This is Pixie.
B: *Pi- What / What's this*?
A: Pixie. P-I-X-I-E.

Discussion box

1 You lose something. You can't find it. Say what happens.

2 Do you have a nickname? Do your friends have nicknames? What are their nicknames?

3 When do you answer the phone for someone?

---

10 Improvisation

Work with a partner. Take two minutes to prepare a short role play. Try to use some of the expressions from Exercise 9a. Do not write the text, just agree on your ideas for a short scene. Then act it out.

Roles: Mark and Jo's mom

Situation: at Meadow Hall on the phone

Basic idea: Jo's mom calls for Jo. Jo's still busy.

Use one of these sentences to start the conversation:

Mark: Hello?

Jo's mom: Hello. May I speak to Jo?

11 Free Time ⊙ DVD Episode 1

a Look at the photo. What are the people doing? Make a short dialogue.

b Match. Then watch Episode 1 and check your answers.

1 A: Hi, Kate. _____e_____
2 A: Good night. _____
3 A: What's your cell number? _____
4 A: Jo? _____
5 A: Do you want to play? _____
6 A: Is it yours? _____

a B: It's 212-645-5960.
b B: Bye!
c B: No, I'm not Jo.
d B: Yes, thanks.
e B: Oh, hi, Mark.
f B: Yeah. Cool!

12 Write

a Read the message. Who is it to?

> To: Lucy
> From: Mrs. Harris
> Phone number: 212-456-2304
> Message: The homework is on page 78.

b Complete the information about the message in Exercise 12a.

This message is to ___Lucy___ . It's from _____ . Her phone number is _____ . The homework is on page _____ .

c Write about this message.

> To: Ron
> From: Joel
> Phone number: 917-292-1345
> Message: The soccer game is at 14 Oak Street.
> This message is to _____
> _____
> _____
> _____

d Create your own message and write about it.

> To: _____
> From: _____
> Phone number: _____
> Message: _____
> _____
> This message is to _____
> _____
> _____
> _____

13 Last but not least: more speaking

Work with a partner. Have a conversation with the messages you wrote in Exercise 12d.

A: *Hello. May I speak to... ?*

B: *She's/He's busy. Can I take a message?*

A: *Yes, this is...*

Check your progress

1 Grammar

a Choose the correct answer.

1 two English _____
   a book (b) books c bookes

2 _____ interesting book
   a it b an c a

3 an _____
   a old desk b desk old c old desks

4 three _____
   a men b man c mans

5 _____ cheap computer
   a it b an c a

6 one _____
   a persons b people c person

   [5]

b Circle the correct answer.

1 It's a (hotel big / big hotel).

2 It's (a / an) old computer.

3 I have three (pen / pens).

4 See the three (childs / children)?

5 It's (a / an) small desk.

6 The opposite of *good* is (bad / big).

7 I want two (hamburger / hamburgers).

8 The opposite of *old* is (cheap / new).

   [7]

c Complete the conversations with the correct words.

morning ~~hey~~ bye Fine, thanks.
Yeah, see you.

1 A: ¹ _____Hey_____, Joe. Good ² _____.

   B: How are you?

   A: ³ _____.

2 A: Bye, Sue.

   B: ⁴ _____, Kate. See you later!

   A: ⁵ _____.

   [4]

2 Vocabulary

a Write the words from the box in four lists.

twenty-five   taxi
café   yellow
~~blue~~   pencil
board   ~~pizza~~
green   sixteen
~~chair~~   red
~~forty-eight~~   four
airport   notebook

Colors	Classroom objects
blue	_chair_
....	....
....	....
....	....

Numbers	International words
forty-eight	_pizza_
....	....
....	....
....	....

   [12]

b Write the letters and words in the correct order.

1 E C D F _____ C, D, E, F

2 six four eight two _____

3 evening afternoon morning night
   _____

4 K H I J _____

5 fifty thirty ten forty _____

6 R P Q O _____

7 Y Z W X _____

   [6]

How did you do?

Check your score.

Total score	😊	😐	😞
[34]	Very good	OK	Not very good
Grammar	16 – 13	12 – 10	9 or less
Vocabulary	18 – 15	14 – 11	10 or less

3 He's a soccer player.

* The verb *be* (singular): statements and questions
* Question words: *Who, What, How old, Where?*
* Vocabulary: countries and nationalities

1 Read and Listen

a ▶ **CD1 T19** Read and listen to the dialogue between Emma and Olivia. Who knows the tennis player's name?

Emma: This line is long, and I'm bored.

Olivia: Emma, look!

Emma: What?

Olivia: Look, there, in the line!

Emma: Where?

Olivia: There! It's that famous tennis player!

Emma: Is it Fernando Torres?

Olivia: No, it isn't! Fernando Torres isn't a tennis player. He's a soccer player.

Emma: Well, who is it? What's his name?

Olivia: It's a Spanish name.

Emma: Kaka?

Olivia: No! Kaka's Brazilian, and he's a soccer player, too.

Emma: Oh, wait ... is it Rafael Nadal?

Olivia: Yes, it is! That's right. He's gorgeous. Who's he with?

Emma: Oh! She's an American actress ... Angelina, um ...

Olivia: Jolie? Angelina Jolie! Wow! Oh. No. Look. She isn't Angelina Jolie.

Emma: No. And look ... he isn't Rafael Nadal. But I'm not bored now! This is fun!

b ▶ CD1 T20 Who are these celebrities? Write the names from the box under the photos. Then listen and check.

Matt Damon   Brad Pitt   Kelly Clarkson   Lily Allen

1 _____ 2 _____ 3 _____ 4 _____

2 Grammar

✱ The verb *be* (singular)

a Look at the examples.

I'm bored.
Is it Rafael Nadal?   Yes, it is.   He isn't a soccer player.

b Complete the table.

Affirmative	Negative	Question	Short answer Affirmative/Negative
I'm (I am.)	I'm not (I am not).	Am I?	Yes, I am. / No, I'm not.
You _____ (You are.)	You **aren't** (**You are not**).	_____ you?	Yes, you _____ . / No, you _____ .
He's (He is.)	He **isn't** (He **is not**).	_____ he?	Yes, he _____ . / No, he **isn't**.
She _____ (She **is**.)	She _____ (She **is not**).	_____ she?	Yes, she _____ . / No, she _____ .
It _____ (It **is**.)	It _____ (It **is not**).	_____ it?	Yes, it _____ . / No, it _____ .

c Write *'m*, *'re* or *'s* in the blanks.

1 I _____ an actor, not a tennis player.
2 He _____ a movie star, not a soccer player.
3 You _____ right, Sue. Good!
4 She _____ a great teacher.

d Write negative sentences.

1 He's from Italy.   *He isn't from Italy.* _____
2 She's a movie star.   _____
3 You're the winner.   _____
4 I'm a tennis player. _____

e Write words from the box in the blanks to make questions.

Is   Are   ~~Am~~   Is

1 *Am* I right?
2 _____ you OK?
3 _____ he the winner?
4 _____ it a big hotel?

f Work with a partner. Ask and answer questions from the box.

How old are you? I'm _____ .
My sister's 12. My best friend is 13.

How old is your sister?
How old is your brother?
How old is your best friend?

LOOK!

You are _____ .
Are you _____ ?

3 Vocabulary

* Countries

a ▶ CD1 T21 Listen and repeat the names of the countries.

●   ●●   ● ●   ● ● ●

Spain   China   Brazil   Canada

●● ●   ● ● ●   ●

South <u>Korea</u>   the <u>United States</u>

b ▶ CD1 T22 Listen and write the countries from the box in the table.

Australia   Mexico   Japan   Colombia
~~Egypt~~   Germany   Britain   Peru

● ●	● ●
Egypt	
● ● ●	● ● ●

c Work with a partner. Match the numbers on the map with the countries in Exercises 3a and 3b.

Number one's _____ .   Is number two _____ ?

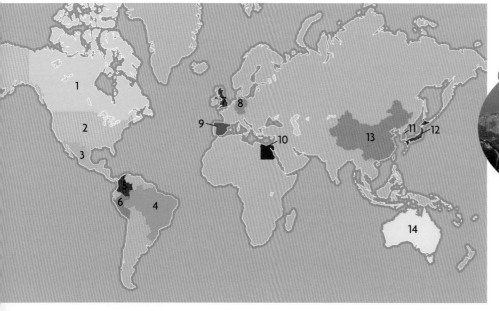

d ▶ CD1 T23 Listen and check.

e Match the countries with the pictures.

I think number one's in _____ .

Egypt   Peru   Britain   Brazil   Japan

4 Grammar

* Where are you from?

a ▶ CD1 T24 Listen and write the words in the blanks.

A: Hi! I'm Andrea. I'm from
   [1] _____ .

B: Hi, Andrea. [2] _____
   Leo.

A: Where are you
   [3] _____ , Leo?

B: Mexico.

b Complete the sentences.

1 I _____ from
  China.

2 Where _____ you
  from?

3 He's _____
  Mexico.

5 Pronunciation

► CD1 T25 Pronunciation section starts on page 114.

6 Vocabulary

✱ Nationalities

a Write the nationality adjectives of these countries in the table.

Egypt ~~Britain~~ ~~Colombia~~ ~~the United States~~
Mexico ~~China~~ Spain Japan

-ian	-an
Colombian	*American*
-ish	**-ese**
British	*Chinese*

b **► CD1 T26** Listen, check and repeat.

c Write the nationalities under the flags.

Canadian British Mexican South Korean
Brazilian American Chinese Spanish

1 _____   2 _____

3 _____   4 _____

5 _____   6 _____

7 _____   8 _____

d Work with a partner.

I think number _____ is the South Korean flag.
What's number _____ ?

e **► CD1 T27** Listen and check.

LOOK!

an American actor / **a Colombian** singer / **a Japanese** writer

7 Grammar

✱ Wh- question words

a How do you say these question words in your language?

What?
Where?
Who?
How old?

b Write the question words from Exercise 7a in the blanks.

1 A: ___*What's*___ this?
  B: It's an Australian flag.

2 A: _____ are you from?
  B: I'm from Miami.

3 A: _____'s this in English?
  B: It's a book.

4 A: _____'s your school?
  B: It's here, in Salvador.

5 A: _____ old are you?
  B: I'm 13.

6 A: _____'s this?
  B: She's my friend.

Heroes

Lionel Messi

Sertab Erener

Ellen Page

Zheng Jie

Usher

Lorena Ochoa

Rodrigo Santoro

8 Speak

Work with a partner. Talk about the people on page 20. Use the information below.

Lorena Ochoa's a golfer. She's from Guadalajara. She's Mexican.

1 ... a pop singer.	... ~~Guadalajara~~.	... ~~Mexican~~.
2 ... an actress.	... Rio de Janeiro.	... Chinese.
3 ... a singer.	... Halifax.	... Turkish.
4 ... a soccer player.	... Rosario.	... Brazilian.
5 ... a tennis player.	... Chengdu.	... Canadian.
6 ... an actor.	... Dallas.	... American.
7 ... ~~a golfer~~.	... Istanbul.	... Argentinian.

9 Listen

a ▶ CD1 T28 Listen and check your answers to Exercise 8.

b Correct the information.

1 Zheng Jie is a golfer. *No, she isn't. She's a tennis player.*

2 Lionel Messi is from Barcelona.

3 Sertab Erener is from London.

4 Lorena Ochoa is Spanish.

5 Rodrigo Santoro is a singer.

6 Ellen Page is from Istanbul.

7 Usher is from Turkey.

c Who is your hero?

10 Write

a Read the example. Where is Joanna from? How old is she? Who is her hero?

Hi! I'm Joanna. I'm 14. I'm American. I'm from San Diego. My address is 14 Market Street, San Diego, California. My cell phone number is 234-215-7029. My hero is Alicia Keys. She's from New York.

This isn't Alicia, this is me!

b Now write about yourself. Use Joanna's text to help you.

Hi!

For your portfolio

4 We're a new band.

* The verb *be* (plural): negatives and questions
* *I (don't) like ... / Do you like ... ?*
* Object pronouns
* Vocabulary: affirmative and negative adjectives

1 Read and listen

a Work with a partner. Name three songs or bands that are popular in your country right now.

Chuck: Hi! It's great to be here today. We're the Targets, and we're a new band. I'm Chuck, the singer. That's Keith on lead guitar, Sandra on bass guitar and Connor on drums. OK ... are there any questions before our first song?

Girl: Yes ... are you all from the same city?

Chuck: Yes, we are.

Sandra: No, we aren't! Chuck, Keith and Connor are all from Newark! I'm from New York City.

Boy: Um ... how old are you?

Keith: Chuck and I are 19, and Sandra and Connor are 18.

Chuck: OK, guys ... This is our first song for you today. It's new, and it's ... "Are We Alone?"

b ▶ CD1 T29 Chuck is the singer in a band. Read and listen to the interview. Then answer the questions.

1 What is the name of the band?
2 How many people are there in the band?

c Read the sentences and write *T* (true) or *F* (false).

1 Keith and Chuck both play the guitar in the band. ☐
2 Two people in the band are not from Newark. ☐
3 Chuck is from New York City. ☐
4 All the people in the band are 18. ☐
5 "Are We Alone?" is an old song. ☐

2 Grammar

✳ The verb *be* (plural): negatives and questions

a Look at the examples.

We're a new band.   We aren't all from Newark.   Are you all from the same city?

b Complete the table.

Affirmative	Negative	Question	Short answer Affirmative / Negative
You're (**You are**).	You **aren't**.	**Are** you?	Yes, you _____ . / No, you _____ .
We _____ (**We are**).	We _____ .	_____ we?	Yes, we. _____ . / No, we _____ .
They _____ (**They are**).	They _____ .	_____ they?	Yes, they. _____ . / No, they _____ .

> ## LOOK!
> The band **is**
> Coldplay **is**
> The Targets **are**

c Write the correct words in the spaces.

1   **Andy:** Are they American?

    Eda: No, they _____ . They _____ British.

2   **Mom:** _____ you and Dave OK?

    Alex: No, we _____ .

3   **Arne:** _____ you from China?

    Aki: No, we _____ . We _____
    from Japan.

d Complete the sentences.

1   **A:** Is Simon Australian?

    B: No, I think _____ British.

2   **A:** Is *Avatar* a good movie?

    B: No, _____ very interesting.

3   **A:** Tokio Hotel? _____ it a pop band?

    B: Yes, it _____ !

4   **A:** _____ Marco and Daniela from Brazil?

    B: No, _____ Brazilian. They're Spanish.

e Look at the pictures and complete the questions.

1   *Are* the Killers a popular band in your country?

2   _____ Daniel Craig British or American?

3   _____ Camden Market in London?

4   _____ Angelina Jolie and Brad Pitt actors?

5   _____ Busch Gardens a theme park in England?

6   _____ Kia a Japanese company?

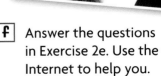

f Answer the questions in Exercise 2e. Use the Internet to help you.

3 Vocabulary

✳ Affirmative and negative adjectives

a Look at the words in the box. Do the words mean *very good* or *very bad*?

> fantastic   excellent   awful   terrible   great

b Work with a partner. Make sentences. Use words in the box.

I think Rio is a fantastic city.

> a fantastic city   a terrible CD   a great band
> an awful restaurant   an excellent team   a terrible movie

4 Grammar and speaking

✳ I (don't) like … / Do you like … ?

a Write the verbs from these sentences in the table.

I *like* the Black Eyed Peas.
I *don't like* Pink.

☺ _____	☹ _____

b Who do you like? Write your answers.

A singer I like: _____
A band I don't like: _____
My favorite band: _____
My favorite singer: _____

Question	Short answer	Statement	Negative
Do you **like** … ?	Yes, I **do.** No, I **don't (do not).**	I **like** …	I **don't like** …

c Work with a partner. Say your answers to Exercise 4b.

I like Miley Cyrus.
I don't like Plain White T's.
My favorite band is Coldplay.
My favorite singer is Justin Timberlake.

d Work with a partner. Ask and answer questions about the pictures. Use the words from the box and the words from Exercise 3a.

> soccer   chocolate   coffee   jam   cats
> classical music   dogs   horses   volleyball

A: *Do you like soccer?*
B: *No, I don't. It's terrible. Do you like volleyball?*
A: *Yes, I do. It's my favorite sport! Do you like cats?*
B: *No, I don't. They're awful!*

5 Grammar

✱ Object pronouns

a ▶ **CD1 T30** Read and listen to the dialogue.

A: *Here's the new Juanes CD. Do you like him?*
B: *He's OK. My favorite band is the Jonas Brothers.*
A: *I don't like them.*

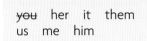

b Write the words from the box in the table.

~~you~~ her it them us me him

Subject:	I	you	she	he	it	we	they
Object:	....	*you*	....	....	....	....	....

c Complete the sentences with words from Exercise 5b.

1 Justin Timberlake is boring. I don't like .... any more.

2 The Targets are my favorite band. I love ....

3 Lily Allen is a really good singer. I like .... a lot.

4 I like Carol and her brother, but they don't like .... !

6 Pronunciation

▶ **CD1 T31, T32 and T33** Pronunciation section starts on page 114.

7 Listen and speak

a ▶ **CD1 T34** Listen to four people talking about the people in the photos. Write the names under *like* or *don't like* in the table.

	like 😊	don't like 🙁
Speaker 1	*Madonna and*	....
Speaker 2	....	....
Speaker 3	....	....
Speaker 4	....	....

b Work with a partner. Talk about celebrities you really like or don't like.

A: *Do you like Jennifer Aniston?*
B: *Yes, I really like her. I think she's fantastic. Do you like Gwyneth Paltrow?*
A: *No, I don't. I think she's awful.*

c ▶ **CD1 T35** Listen and complete the song lyrics with the correct forms of *be*.

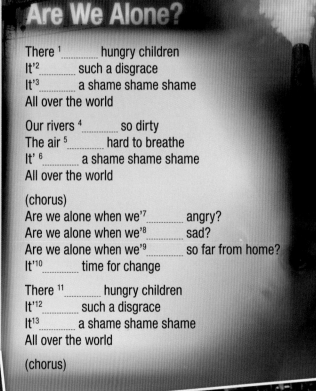

Are We Alone?

There ¹ .... hungry children
It'² .... such a disgrace
It'³ .... a shame shame shame
All over the world

Our rivers ⁴ .... so dirty
The air ⁵ .... hard to breathe
It' ⁶ .... a shame shame shame
All over the world

(chorus)
Are we alone when we'⁷ .... angry?
Are we alone when we'⁸ .... sad?
Are we alone when we'⁹ .... so far from home?
It'¹⁰ .... time for change

There ¹¹ .... hungry children
It'¹² .... such a disgrace
It¹³ .... a shame shame shame
All over the world

(chorus)

Just a little joke

8 Read and listen

a ▶ CD1 T36 Look at the title of the story and the pictures. Who is on the phone with Mark? Read, listen and check.

1

Darren: Hey, girls! There's a Targets concert here, at the center!

Izzie: The Targets? Really? They're a great band!

Darren: That's right, The Targets! They're my friends.

Kate: Cool! When's the concert?

Darren: Saturday.

2

Darren: Do you want to go? Together?

Izzie: Of course!

Kate: Absolutely! They're my favorite band.

3

Mark: Darren, it's for you. It's your friend Chuck, the singer from the Targets.

Darren: Oh. Um. OK, look. There's no concert ... sorry! Just a little joke. I'm sorry, guys.

4

Mark: I know, Darren. And it isn't Chuck on the phone. Just a little joke, too!

b Read the story again. Mark the statements *T* (true) or *F* (false).

1 The Targets' concert is at the youth center. T

2 The concert is on Friday night. F

3 Izzie wants to go, but Kate doesn't want to go. F

4 Chuck is the singer from The Targets. T

5 Chuck is on the phone with Mark. F

9 Everyday English

a Find the expressions in the story. Who says them?

1 Cool!   ....

2 Of course! ....

3 I'm sorry ... .

4 I know ...   .

b How do you say the expressions in Exercise 9a in your language?

c ▶ CD1 T37 Read the dialogue and put the sentences in the correct order. Then listen and check.

[ ] **Alex:** Together? OK, cool! Let's go on Friday.

[1] **Alex:** The new *Matrix* movie is at the movie theater this weekend.

[ ] **Alex:** No problem! Is Saturday OK?

[6] **Sally:** Of course! Saturday's great. See you there!

[ ] **Sally:** I know. And *Matrix* movies are great! Let's go together!

[ ] **Sally:** Oh, Alex, I'm sorry, not Friday. It's my mom's birthday.

d Underline the correct options.

1 A: Let's go to the café on Saturday.

   B: Saturday? *Cool! / I'm sorry.* Saturday's great!

2 A: Do you like pizza?

   B: *I know / Of course.* Pizza's fantastic.

3 A: Marsha, let's go to the hamburger place.

   B: The hamburger place? *I'm sorry / Of course,* Mike. I don't like hamburgers.

4 A: Jennifer Hudson's a great singer.

   B: *I know / I'm sorry.* I think she's really good, too.

10 Improvisation

Work with a partner. Take two minutes to prepare a short role play. Try to use some of the expressions from Exercise 9a. Do not write the text, just agree on your ideas for a short scene. Then act it out.

Roles: Darren and Izzie

Situation: At school, a week later

Basic idea: Darren has an idea. There is a soccer game on Sunday. Soccer is his favorite sport. Izzie is not very happy.

11 Free Time ⊙ DVD Episode 2

a Who are the two people? Where are they? Make a short dialogue for the people in the photo.

b Match the pictures with the speech bubbles.

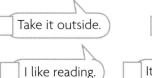 Take it outside.

Throw the ball.

I like reading.

It's fantastic. You're amazing.

12 Write

a Read Anna's email about her favorite band.
What is her favorite CD?

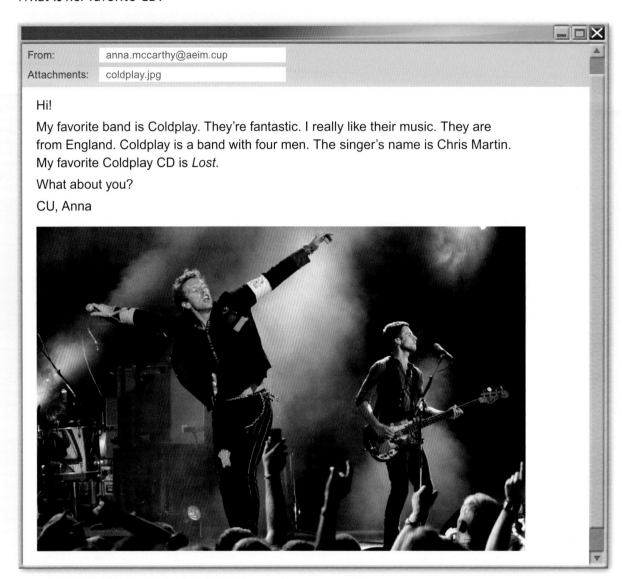

From: anna.mccarthy@aeim.cup

Attachments: coldplay.jpg

Hi!

My favorite band is Coldplay. They're fantastic. I really like their music. They are from England. Coldplay is a band with four men. The singer's name is Chris Martin. My favorite Coldplay CD is *Lost*.

What about you?

CU, Anna

b Write your friend an email about your favorite band. Tell him or her:

- the name of your favorite band
- where they are from
- why you like them
- who is in the band

Use Anna's email to help you.

13 Last but not least: more speaking

a Cut out photos of celebrities from a magazine. In pairs, think of questions you would like to ask the star. Also think what you would like to tell him/her in English.

b One of you comes to the front. He or she is the celebrity in the photo. He or she holds the photo of the famous person. The others ask questions.

What's your (favorite) ...?   *How old ...?*

Where ...?   *Are you ...?*

Do you (like) ...?   *We really like ...*

We think ...

Check your progress

1 Grammar

a Write the words in the correct order.

1 am / I / an / town / old / from / Spain / in

   I am from an old town in Spain.

2 are / friends / great / singers / My

   _____

3 fantastic / San Diego / a / city / is

   _____

4 really / are / restaurants / Japanese / good

   _____

   [ ] 3

b Write the words from the box in the blanks.

> ~~Do~~ Are Do don't
> don't isn't Is aren't

1 _Do_ you like soccer?

2 My friends _____ like U2.

3 _____ you from the U.S.?

4 She _____ Mexican, she's Peruvian.

5 _____ your brothers like music?

6 _____ Julia Roberts Australian?

7 They _____ British, they're American!

8 My mother and father _____ like pop music!

   [ ] 7

c Write the question words from the box in the blanks.

> ~~What~~ Where Who How What

1 A: _What_ is this?

   B: It's a Brazilian flag.

2 A: _____ old is your brother?

   B: He's 14.

3 A: _____ is your English teacher?

   B: Mrs. Wells.

4 A: _____ are your names?

   B: I'm Claire, and this is Kate.

5 A: _____ are you from?

   B: I'm from Egypt.

   [ ] 4

2 Vocabulary

a Write the countries.

1 M _E_ _X_ _I_ _C_ O

2 B _ _ _ _ L

3 B _ _ _ _ _ _ N

4 S _ _ _ H K _ _ _ A

5 S _ _ _ N

6 A _ _ _ _ _ _ _ A

7 J _ _ _ N

8 C _ _ _ _ A

   [ ] 7

b Write the nationalities for people from the countries in Exercise 2a.

1 _Mexican_

2 _____

3 _____

4 _____

5 _____

6 _____

7 _____

8 _____

   [ ] 7

c Underline the correct adjective in each sentence.

1 I like this book. It's *awful / great*.

2 A: Do you like Paris?

   B: Yes, it's a *fantastic / terrible* city.

3 A: This movie is not very good.

   B: Yes, you're right. It's *awful / fantastic*.

4 We don't like the pizza. It's *great / terrible*.

   [ ] 4

How did you do?

Check your score.

Total score		😐	☹
[32]	Very good	OK	Not very good
Grammar	14 – 11	10 – 9	8 or less
Vocabulary	18 – 15	14 – 11	10 or less

* Simple present: affirmative and negative; questions and short answers
* Possessive 's; possessive adjectives
* Vocabulary: family

1 Read and listen

a Look at the photos. Who is the woman? Read the magazine article and check your answer.

America's First Lady

Michelle Obama is America's First Lady, the wife of the U.S. president, Barack Obama. Millions see her on TV. What do you know about her? Where is she from? How does she live?

Mrs. Obama is from Chicago. She's the daughter of Fraser and Marian Robinson. Her father is dead, and Marian doesn't live in Chicago anymore. Marian is an important woman now. She is the grandmother of President Obama's children.

Now the First Lady and her family live in Washington, D.C., in the White House. There are 132 rooms and 35 bathrooms – but Mrs. Obama and her family don't use them all!

The Obamas live with Michelle Obama's mother, their two daughters, Malia and Sasha, and their dog, Bo. Bo, a present to the girls from their father, is a Portuguese water dog.

The First Lady is very busy. She works on important projects for the American people. She also helps her husband with his work and his official duties.

b ▶ CD1 T38 Read the article again and listen. Write *T* (true) or *F* (false).

1 Michelle Obama is from England. [F]
2 Her mother is alive, but her father isn't. [T]
3 Her mother's name is Fraser. [F]
4 Mrs. Obama lives in Chicago now. [F]
5 There are two girls in the Obama family. [T]
6 Mrs. Obama helps her husband with his work. [T]

c What do you know about the president of the U.S.?

2 Grammar

⭐ Simple present: affirmative and negative

a Look at the sentences. <u>Underline</u> the verbs.

1 Millions <u>see</u> her on TV.
2 She doesn't <u>live</u> in Chicago.
3 She <u>helps</u> her husband.
4 They don't <u>use</u> all the rooms in the White House.

b Complete the table.

Affirmative	Negative
I / you / we / they _read_.	I / you / we / they _don't_ read.
He / she (it) reads.	He/she/ (it) _doesn't_ read.

c Look at the spelling for the third person singular. Complete the table.

+s	+es	+ies
learn → learns	watch → watches	study → studies
stop → _stops_	finish → _finishes_	
live → _lives_	go → _goes_	
play → _plays_		

d Write the correct words in the blanks.

1 I ___like___ cats. (like)
2 We _don't like_ pizza. (not like)
3 He _studies_ French at school. (study)
4 He _don't speaks_ Korean. (not speak)
5 She _don't listen_ to music. (not listen)
6 I _don't studies_ English. (not study)

⭐ Simple present: questions and short answers

e Look at these questions in the simple present.

What **do you know** about her? _She is the First Lady_
Do they live in the White House? _Obama, Michele, Marian, Malia sasha and boo . Do_
Does she have a dog? _Yes, Bo . Bo_
Do they use all the rooms? _No, they don't_

f Complete the table with *do* or *does*.

Question	Short answer	
	Affirmative	Negative
Does he/she speak Korean?	Yes, he/she _does_.	No, he/she **doesn't (does not)**.
_Do_ I/you/we/they study English?	Yes, I/you/we/they _do_.	No, I/you/we/they _don't_.

9 Complete the sentences with *Do* or *Does*.

1 ___Do___ people see Michelle Obama on TV?
2 _____ Michelle Obama live with her mother?
3 _____ Malia and Sasha like their dog Bo?
4 _____ President Obama have a lot of official duties?
5 _____ Michelle and Barack Obama live in Washington, D.C.?

3 Pronunciation

▶ **CD1 T39** Pronunciation section starts on page 114.

4 Speak

a Work with a partner. Ask the questions in Exercise 2g and use short answers.

A: *Do people see Michelle Obama on TV?*
B: *Yes, they do.*

b Make questions. Then ask your partner.

1 Do you watch   _4_   a the newspaper?
2 Do you study   _____   b volleyball?
3 Do you play   _____   c French at school?
4 Do you read   _____   d pop music?
5 Do you listen to   _____   e cartoons on TV?

c Make sentences about your partner. Tell other students.

David doesn't watch cartoons on TV.
He studies French at school. He …

5 Vocabulary

✱ Family

a Write the words from the box in the blanks. Check your answers with the magazine article on page 30.

> daughters   father   sister
> mother   grandmother

1 Michelle Obama's _____ is dead.

2 Her _____ lives in the White House.

3 Marian is Malia and Sasha's _____ .

4 Mrs. Obama's _____ are Malia and Sasha.

5 Malia is Sasha's _____ .

b ▶ CD1 T40 Look at Sally's family tree. Write the words from the box in the blanks. Then listen and check your answers.

> cousin   mother   father
> uncle   aunt   ~~grandfather~~
> brother   sister   grandmother

Sally's family

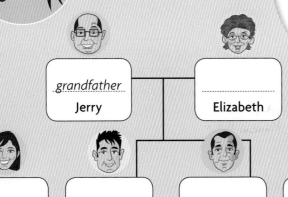

grandfather
Jerry

_____
Elizabeth

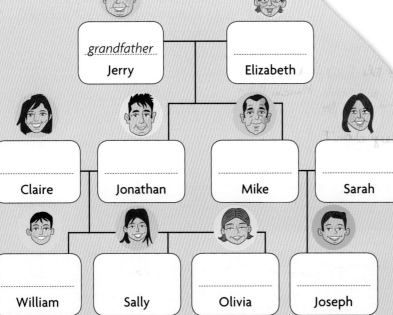

_____
Claire

_____
Jonathan

_____
Mike

_____
Sarah

_____
William

_____
Sally

_____
Olivia

_____
Joseph

6 Grammar

✱ Possessive 's

a Look at the examples.

My father's name is Jonathan, and my mother's name is Claire.

My grandmother and grandfather are my father's parents.

b Look at the pictures and write the correct words with 's.

Daniel

Emily

1 _____ *Daniel's book* _____   2 _____

Mr. Black

My father

3 _____   4 _____

My sister

5 _____

My brother

6 _____

✳ Possessive adjectives

c Look at the examples.

Their dog Bo is a Portuguese water dog.
She helps *her* husband with *his* work.

d Complete the table.

Singular	I _____	you _____	she **her**	he _____	it _____
Plural	we **our**	you _____	they _____		

e Write words from Exercise 6d in the blanks.

1 Hi! ___My___ name's Natalie. Nice to meet you. What's _____ name?

2 My brother really likes music. _____ favorite singer is Jay-Z.

3 I have two sisters. _____ names are Laura and Joanna.

4 Amy's American. She's in England with _____ family.

5 We live in London now, but we don't really like _____ house.

6 Do you and your sister like _____ new house?

⑦ Speak

a Work with a partner. Look at Sally's family tree on page 32. Ask and answer questions about her family.

A: *Who's Jonathan?*
B: *He's Sally's father.*
B: *Is Joseph Sally's brother?*
A: *No, he isn't. He's her cousin.*

b Draw your family tree. Write *father*, *mother*, etc., but not their names!

c Work with a partner. Exchange your family trees and fill in the names.

My mother's name is Gabriela, and my father's name is Manuel. My sister's name is ...

⑧ Listen

a Match the verbs with the pictures. Write 1–6 in the boxes.

1 go to the Internet café
2 go to the movies
3 work in a bakery
4 go to museums
5 go bowling
6 go shopping

b ▶ CD1 T41 Listen to the dialogue between Paul and Ben. Then look at the pictures and write *A–F* in the correct order.

___D___ _____ _____ _____ _____ _____

9 Read and listen

a Read about two American families. Where is each family from?

★American families

1

The Gomez family lives in El Paso, Texas. El Paso is a big city in the southwestern part of Texas, near Mexico. Manuel is American, but his wife, Gabriela, is from Mexico. They have two young children, Danilo and Claudia. The four of them live with Manuel's mother and father. Manuel's cousin lives on the same street.

The family has a small store. They sell newspapers and magazines. They live in a large apartment above the store. Manuel and his cousin work in the store, but Gabriela doesn't. She teaches Spanish at a high school in El Paso. During the day, Manuel's parents take care of Danilo and Claudia. At night, everyone eats dinner together at home.

2

The Wilson family lives in Tampa, Florida. Jenna Wilson works part-time at a hospital. She's a nurse. Her husband, Mark, works in a factory. Jenna and Mark have three teenage children. Kevin is 14, Mark is 16 and Lilly is 17.

The Wilsons rent a house, but they want to buy their own house one day. So, they save money when they can. For example, they don't go to the movies. They watch movies at home. It saves a lot of money.

The Wilsons' three teenage children are in a band. They practice their music in the basement after school every day.

b ▶ CD1 T42 Complete the missing information in the table. Then listen and check your answers.

Family	City	Number of children	Mother's job	Father's job
the Gomez family	El Paso			
the Wilson family				

c Are families different in different parts of your country?

10 Write

a Read Natalie's webpage about her family. Write names under the pictures.

Hi, I'm Natalie Walker.
I'm 15, and I live in Chicago.
It's a fantastic city.

This is my sister, Keisha. She's 13. We go shopping together on the weekend. My brother, Andrew, is 18. He works in a store downtown. He's OK, but sometimes we fight.

This is my father. His name's Jared, and he's 44. He's a teacher. My mother's name is Donna. She's 44, too, and she works in a bank. My grandparents' names are Clarence and Janice. They're great! They live in Chicago, too.

1 _____Natalie_____ 2 _____ 3 _____

4 _____ 5 _____ 6 _____

b Write a paragraph about your family. Use Natalie's webpage to help you.

For your portfolio

6 Where's the market?

* there's / there are
* Affirmative imperatives
* Prepositions of place
* Vocabulary: places in towns, numbers 100 +

1 Read and listen

▶ **CD1 T43** Read the webpage and match the pictures and the paragraphs. Write a–f in the boxes. Then read the web page again and listen.

Things to see and do in Boston

1 There's an underground subway system in Boston. It's called the T. You can get to many places in Boston using the T. There are five lines – red, green, orange, blue and silver. One of the T lines is over 109 years old. ☐

2 Go to Fenway Park and see a baseball game. The Boston Red Sox play at the stadium. It has almost 37,000 seats! ☐

3 Walk the Freedom Trail in downtown Boston. There are 16 famous sites. See Paul Revere's House or the Bunker Hill Monument. Paul Revere's House is over 330 years old. It's the oldest house in Boston. Take a tour, or walk the trail on your own. ☐

4 Do you want to buy clothes or other items? There's a great market called Faneuil Hall Marketplace. It's been in Boston for over 250 years. There are more than 100 places to shop. There's food, too. Seventeen restaurants and 40 carts sell food. ☐

5 You can visit many interesting museums in Boston. Visit the Museum of Science, for example. There are over 500 exhibits there. ☐

6 Do you like music? Go to a concert! There are different concerts every day. Or watch dancers at the Boston Ballet. ☐

2 Vocabulary

✱ Numbers 100 +

▶ **CD1 T44** **Listen and repeat the numbers.**

120	a/one hundred and twenty	500	five hundred
150	a/one hundred and fifty	1,000	a/one thousand
200	two hundred	2,000	two thousand
300	three hundred		

3 Pronunciation

▶ **CD1 T45** **Pronunciation section starts on page 114.**

4 Grammar

✱ there's / there are

a Look at the examples. Then complete the table and the rule.

There's an underground subway system in Boston.
There are over 500 exhibits.
Is there a lot to do in Boston?
Are there any interesting museums?

	Singular nouns	Plural nouns
Affirmative	There**'s a** market.	There _____ 500 exhibits.
Negative	There **isn't a** museum.	There **aren't any** concerts.
Questions	**Is there a** market?	_____ there **any** science exhibits?
Short answers	Yes, there _____ . No, there **isn't**.	Yes, there _____ . No, there _____ .

RULE: *There* _____ *a/an* + singular nouns. *There* _____ + plural nouns. Use *any* in _____ and negative sentences with plural nouns.

b Complete the sentences. Use *There's / There isn't* or *There are / aren't any*.

1 __*There's*__ a big park in Boston called Boston Common. ✔
2 __*There aren't any*__ good concerts tonight. ✘
3 _____ interesting exhibits in the Museum of Science. ✔
4 _____ a table for us in the restaurant right now. ✘
5 _____ a concert on Friday. ✔
6 _____ T stops on this street. ✘
7 _____ good restaurants here. ✘
8 _____ a professional baseball team in Boston. ✔

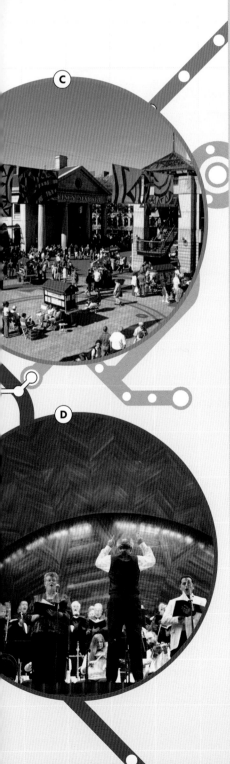

5 Vocabulary

✱ Places in towns

a ▶ **CD1 T46** Write the names of the places under the pictures. Then listen, check and repeat.

~~library~~ bank park bookstore newsstand drugstore post office train station supermarket

1 _____library_____

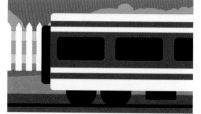

2 _____

3 _____

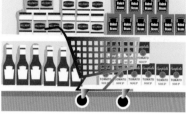

4 _____

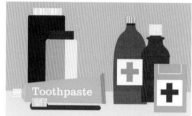

5 _____

6 _____

7 _____

8 _____

9 _____

b Work with a partner. Make questions about your town or city.

A: *Is there a museum in your town?*

B: *Yes, there is. Are there any good bookstores in your town?*

c Where do you do these things?

You buy shampoo in a drugstore or supermarket.

1 buy shampoo
2 send a package
3 catch a train
4 buy stamps
5 change money
6 buy milk
7 play soccer
8 buy a magazine

6 Grammar

✱ Affirmative imperatives

a Look at the examples and the rule.

Go on a Big Bus tour!
Come to the Hard Rock Café and try the food.

> **RULE:** Use the base form of the verb (infinitive without *to*)

b Match the two parts of the sentences.

1 Change   _f_   a to your teacher.
2 Buy   _____   b stamps here.
3 Watch   _____   c for travel cards here.
4 Listen   _____   d down, please.
5 Pay   _____   e this movie, it's great!
6 Sit   _____   f money here.

c Listen to your teacher's instructions.

7 Read and listen

✱ Directions

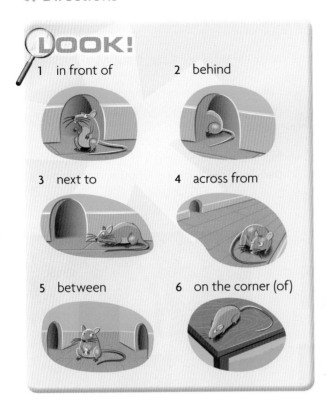

LOOK!

1 in front of
2 behind
3 next to
4 across from
5 between
6 on the corner (of)

▶ **CD1 T47** Two people ask for directions. Read and listen. Then write the names of the places on the map.

Tourist 1: Excuse me, where's the post office, please?

Man: It's on State Street, next to Wilson's, the big bookstore.

Tourist 1: And ... where's State Street? Is it far?

Man: No, it isn't far. Go straight down here to the bank on the corner, and then turn right. That's State Street, and the post office is there on the left.

Tourist 1: Thanks very much!

Man: You're welcome.

Tourist 2: Excuse me, is the train station near here?

Man: Yes, it is. Go straight down this street. Cross State Street. The train station is on the left across from the park.

Tourist 2: Thank you.

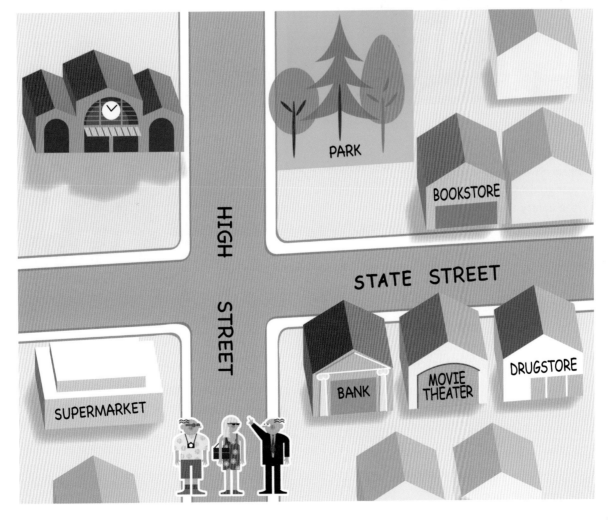

HIGH STREET

STATE STREET

PARK

BOOKSTORE

SUPERMARKET

BANK

MOVIE THEATER

DRUGSTORE

A charity run

8 Read and listen

a ▶ **CD1 T48** Look at the title of the story and the pictures. Why are Kate, Izzie, Mark and Darren late? Read, listen and check.

1

Darren: Jo's in a half-marathon tomorrow for a charity that helps children.

Kate: Really? Great! Let's go and watch her.

Darren: OK – but it's in Clinton. It starts in Riverside Park at 11:00.

2

The next day ...

Izzie: It's 10:50! We're late!

Mark: Wait a minute. Where are we?

Darren: I have no idea!

3

Kate: Excuse me. Where's Riverside Park?

Woman: Riverside Park? Oh, just go down there, past the library and turn left. It's across from the post office.

Kate: Great. Thanks.

Mark: Hurry up! It starts in ten minutes.

4

Mark: Here we are! And look – there's Jo!

Izzie: Hi, Jo. We're here! Good luck!

Jo: Thanks, but actually, the race is over! It started at 8:00.

Darren: Oh, no! Wrong time, sorry!

Jo: It's OK guys. I'm happy you're here!

b Read the story again. Match the beginnings and endings.

1 Jo is in ☐	a	for directions to Riverside Park.
2 The four friends ☐	b	the race is finished.
3 They think the race charts ☐	c	a half-marathon race.
4 They ask a woman ☐	d	to see the four friends.
5 When they get to the park, ☐	e	want to go and watch the race.
6 Jo is very happy ☐	f	at 11 o'clock.

9 Everyday English

a Find the expressions in the story. Who says them?

1   Really? ....

2   Wait a minute. ....

3   I have no idea. ....

4   ... actually, ...

b How do you say each of the expressions in Exercise 9a in your language?

c ► CD1 T49 Read the dialogue and put the sentences in the correct order. Then listen and check.

☐ **Dan:** I have no idea. Let's look at the map again.

6 **Dan:** Good. Now ...

☐ **Dan:** Well, actually Julie, that's the wrong map.

1 **Julie:** Where are we, Dan?

☐ **Julie:** Really? Oh yes. I'm sorry. Wait a minute. OK, here's the right map.

☐ **Julie:** OK. The map's in my backpack. Here it is.

d Fill in each blank with an expression from Exercise 9a.

1   A: I love the Flaming Lips. They're great.

    B: ....? I don't like them at all!

2   A: I have a DVD of a great movie. Let's watch it.

    B: Well, ..., I'm very tired. Can we watch it tomorrow?

3   A: Paula, who's that boy over there?

    B: .... Let's go and ask his name!

4   A: Where's the park?

    B: I don't know. .... Look! I think that's the park, over there!

10 Improvisation

Work in groups of four. Take two minutes to prepare a short role play. Try to use some of the expressions from Exercise 9a. Do not write the text, just agree on your ideas for a short scene. Then act it out.

Roles: Kate, Izzie, Mark and Darren

Situation: In a café

Basic idea: The four friends are in a café. They have their favorite drinks. One of them has an idea. There is a great movie playing at the movie theater. The others like the idea. But then something happens ... and they're late!

11 Free Time ⊙ DVD Episode 3

a Where are they? Who are they? Make a short dialogue.

b Look at the photo of Mark and Darren in the DVD episode. Guess the answers.

1   Who's a fan of classical music?

2   Who's a fan of pop music?

3   Who's angry?

4   What's the problem?

5   Who plays a trick?

12 Write

a Read Rob's text about Princeton.
Match topics 1–3 with the paragraphs.
Write A, B and C in the boxes.

1 The stores and the restaurants ☐

2 Things to see in the city ☐

3 Rob's opinion of Princeton ☐

A I'm from Princeton. It's a beautiful city with a very old university. There are fantastic old and new buildings downtown, and there's a very big park called Community Park. There's also a big university library and there are a few museums.

B There are interesting stores, but there aren't any really big street markets. New York City is only one hour by train, so I go shopping in New York, too. There are good cafés in Princeton. My favorite café is Italian. I like Italian coffee and food a lot!

C Princeton is great. I really like it here!

Rob

b Write a short text about your town or city. Use Rob's text to help you.

13 Last but not least: more speaking

Work together in groups of four. Make a short play.
Roles: three tourists and one local person (a person from <u>your</u> town)
Basic idea:

1 Each tourist thinks of one place they would like to see (for example, the museum).

2 The local person is in a café. One tourist arrives and asks the local person the way (for example, to the museum). The local person tells him/her the *wrong* way. The tourist says "Thank you" and leaves.

3 Then the next tourist arrives and asks for the way (for example, to the post office). The local person tells him/her the wrong way (etc.).

4 In the end, all three tourists meet. They talk about their problem. Suddenly they see the local person …

Check your progress

1 Grammar

a Write the words from the box in the blanks.

> my ~~his~~ her our their your

1 Antonio's father is Canadian, but _____his_____ mother is Italian.

2 We live in Rochester now, but my brother and I don't like _____ new school.

3 **A:** Hello, _____ name's Christine. What's _____ name?

   B: Hi, I'm Caroline.

4 Karen has a really nice sister. _____ name's Patricia.

5 Jackie and Ethan live in Tampa now, but _____ sons are still in Miami.

| 5 |

b Write the correct words in the blanks.

1 He ___studies___ Spanish at school. (study)

2 She _____ English and Italian. (speak)

3 We _____ TV on the weekend. (watch)

4 He _____ his homework before dinner. (finish)

5 My friend _____ to tap dance classes. (go)

6 They _____ to music in their room. (listen)

| 5 |

c Complete the sentences about Boston. Use *There are / Are there / There's / Is there.*

1 ___There are___ over 40 museums in Boston.

2 _____ a great monument on the Freedom Trail.

3 _____ riverboat tours every day.

4 _____ a post office on Franklin Street?

5 _____ any parks in Boston?

6 _____ any good stores at Faneuil Hall Marketplace?

| 5 |

2 Vocabulary

a Write the words from the box in three lists.

> market   drugstore   twenty-one   ~~son~~
> parents   aunt   train station   father
> bookstore   post office   fourteen   ~~fifty~~
> daughter   cousin   newsstand   uncle
> thirteen   seventy   library   eight
> mother   two   thirty   ~~supermarket~~

Places in towns

supermarket   _____

_____   _____

_____   _____

_____

Family

son   _____

_____   _____

_____   _____

_____

Numbers

fifty   _____

_____   _____

_____   _____

| 21 |

b Write the numbers.

1 67   ___sixty-seven___

2 1,000   _____

3 84   _____

4 13   _____

5 19   _____

6 100   _____

7 90   _____

| 6 |

How did you do?

Check your score.

Total score	☺	☺	☹
42	Very good	OK	Not very good
Grammar	15 – 12	11 – 9	8 or less
Vocabulary	27 – 22	21 – 16	15 or less

7 They have brown eyes.

* has/have
* Why ... ? Because ...
* Vocabulary: parts of the body

1 Read and listen

a Read the text. Who is Sally? Who is Paula? Write *Sally* or *Paula* under the pictures.

human DNA

chimp DNA

SALLY OR PAULA?

She's four years old. She's intelligent. She has dark brown hair and brown eyes. She has a small nose and a big smile. She has four fingers and a thumb on her hand.

She lives with her family. She doesn't have a big family. She has two sisters. She likes people, and she loves her sisters and her friends. When she's happy, she jumps up and down and laughs. She loves chocolate and bananas, too!

Is it Sally or Paula? Well, it's both Sally and Paula. Paula's a little girl, and Sally's a chimpanzee. How are they different? Chimpanzees live in forests in Africa, and people live in towns and cities. Why are they similar? Because they have almost the same DNA. DNA is the chemical in our bodies that makes us people, or chimpanzees, or fish, or dogs, and so on. Ninety-eight percent of human DNA and chimpanzee DNA is the same. There's only a 2% difference.

b ▶ CD1 T50 Now read the text again and listen. Write *T* (true) or *F* (false).

1 Sally and Paula have big families.   `F`
2 Paula has two sisters.
3 Sally doesn't like her sisters.
4 People and chimpanzees have very different DNA.

2 Grammar

✳ *Why ...? Because ...*

a Look at the text on page 44 again and the example. Then answer the question.

Why are chimpanzees and people similar? *Because* they have similar DNA.

Why is Sally happy when she eats chocolate? _____ .

✳ *has/have*

b Look at the examples. Then complete the table.

She has four fingers and a thumb on her hand.
She doesn't have a big family.
They have similar DNA.

Affirmative	Negative	Question	Short answer
I/you/we/they **have**.	I/you/we/they _____ (do not) have.	**Do** you/we/they **have**?	Yes, I/you/we/they _____ . No, I/you/we/they _____ (do not).
He/she/it **has**.	He/she/it **doesn't** (does not) have.	_____ he/she/it **have**?	Yes, he/she/it _____ . No, he/she/it _____ (does not).

c Complete the sentences with the correct form of *have* (not).

1 ___Do___ you ___have___ a new camera?

2 My aunt _____ a house in the country. I often go and see her on weekends.

3 Let's watch a DVD. I _____ lots of them.

4 _____ your brother _____ a bike?

5 They _____ a new drummer in their band. She's great.

6 This computer is too expensive for me. I _____ enough money to buy it.

7 _____ they _____ a dog?

8 I _____ your phone number. Can you tell me what it is?

d Make true sentences about you and your family. Use the correct form of *have (not)*.

1 I _____ a big family.

2 My family _____ a big house.

3 My best friend _____ a brother.

4 I _____ a bicycle.

5 I _____ a computer.

6 I _____ a sister.

3 Pronunciation

▶ **CD1 T51 and T52** Pronunciation section starts on page 114.

4 Speak

Work with a partner. Ask and answer questions with *have*.

A: *Do you have a big family?*   B: *No, I don't. Do you have ... ?*

Vocabulary

✱ Parts of the body

▶ **CD1 T53**   Write the words from the box in the blanks. Then listen, check and repeat.

> hand   leg   finger   arm   foot   thumb   mouth   ear   nose   face   hair   eye

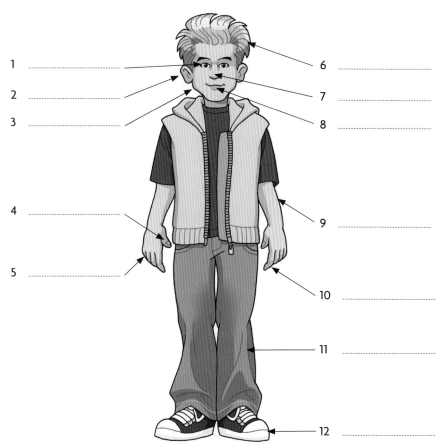

1 ....

2 ....

3 ....

4 ....

5 ....

6 ....

7 ....

8 ....

9 ....

10 ....

11 ....

12 ....

Robert Pattinson

Kate Winslet

⑥ # Listen and speak

✱ Describing people

a   ▶ **CD1 T54**   Write the words in the box in the correct lists. Then listen, check and repeat.

> ~~blonde~~   ~~brown~~ (x2)   short   red   blue   gray (x2)   ~~straight~~
> curly   wavy   medium-length   green   black   long

Hair color	Hair style	Eye color
blonde	*straight*	*brown*
....	....	....
....	....	....
....	....	....
....	....	
	....	

Beyoncé

b   Use the words in the box to describe the people in the pictures.

A: *Robert Pattinson has blue eyes.*

B: *Kate Winslet has long, wavy hair.*

Josh Hartnett

7 Listen and speak

✱ Describing people

a ▶ CD1 T55 Listen to the descriptions of three of the people in the pictures. Check (✔) the pictures of the people they describe.

① 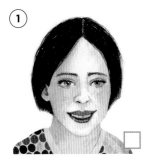 ☐

② 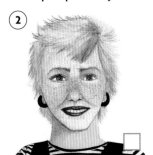 ☐

③ 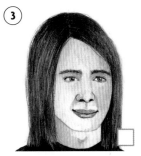 ☐

④ 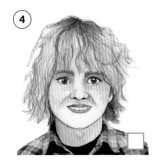 ☐

b Find a picture of a person in this book. Don't show your partner. Describe the person. Your partner says who it is.

A: *He's good-looking. He has short dark hair and brown eyes. He has a nice smile.*

B: *Is it … ?*

✱ Giving personal information

c ▶ CD1 T56 Nina wants to work at Clinton Dog Care. Listen and complete the form.

APPLICATION FORM

Clinton Dog Care

First name: _____ *Nina* _____

Last name: _____

Age: _____

Address: _____

Phone: _____

Cell phone: _____

d Put the words in order to make questions.

1 old / you / are / How   *How old are you* _____ ?

2 name / first / your / What's   _____ ?

3 spell / How / you / do / please / that   _____ ?

4 your / What's / address   _____ ?

5 you / that / Can / repeat / please   _____ ?

6 number / please / telephone / your / What's   _____ ?

e Work with a partner. Ask and answer questions from Exercise 7d.

What's your first name?

How do you spell that, please?

Culture in mind

8 Read and listen

a Read the magazine article. Which pets are popular in the United States?

Different cultures – different pets

Many people have pets in the U.S. About 40% of homes have a dog, and 33% have a cat. Many of these people have more than one cat or dog. Other popular pets in the U.S. are birds, fish, hamsters and rabbits.

fish

But people in other countries have different ideas about pets. In Arab countries, for example, dogs usually aren't popular because people believe they aren't clean. And in Africa, very few people have animals as pets.

fighting cricket

dog

Some people in China and Japan have small but noisy pets. They aren't dogs, cats, fish or birds: they're fighting crickets. These pets are very noisy!

The Inuit of northern Canada have dogs as pets. Their dogs also have a job. They pull sleds that help people get around in the snow.

cat

hamster

rabbit

sled dog

bird

kangaroo

Madagascar hissing cockroach

Another example of an unusual pet is the Madagascar hissing cockroach. It's pretty big. It's clean and doesn't bite, and it sometimes makes a loud noise. Madagascar hissing cockroaches make good pets for children. In Australia and Indonesia, some people have sugar gliders. They are marsupials. These animals have a pocket or pouch for their babies. (A kangaroo is another marsupial.) Sugar gliders "fly" from tree to tree.

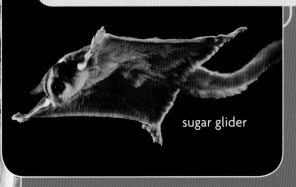

sugar glider

b ▶ **CD1 T57** Read the text again and listen. Answer the questions.

1 Which two pets are noisy?
2 Where aren't dogs popular?
3 Where do people have crickets as pets?
4 Where do people have sled dogs as pets?
5 Do hissing cockroaches bite?
6 What do kangaroos and sugar gliders both have?

c What pets are popular in your country?

9 Write

a Read Anna's descriptions of her brother and her best friend. Match the descriptions with the pictures. Write the numbers in the boxes.

> 1 My brother's name is Matt, and he's 15. He wears glasses, and he has brown eyes and short blonde hair. He really likes music. His favorite band is Rise Against.
>
> 2 My best friend's name is David, and he's 14. He's from Brazil, but he lives in London. He's good-looking, and he has short brown hair and green eyes. He has a pet dog named Luc. He likes sports, and he plays tennis and soccer.

A

B

b Write two short descriptions of your friends or family. Use Anna's texts to help you.

This is delicious!

* *I'd like / Would you like ... ?*
* Count and noncount nouns

* this/that/these/those
* Vocabulary: food

1 Read and listen

a Look at the pictures. Then write the words in the chart.

alligator crickets eggs
sushi grasshopper
snake

Raw food	Reptiles	Insects
eggs		

b ▶ CD1 T58 Read the article and listen. Check your answers to Exercise 1a.

Unusual food around the world

Raw food

Some people think that meat, fish and eggs need to be cooked. This isn't always true. There is raw fish in many Japanese dishes, such as sushi. People also put raw eggs on rice in Japan. In the U.S., raw egg is used in Caesar salads. Steak tartare, raw beef, is popular in many countries in Europe.

Reptiles

Beef, chicken and fish are usual meats people eat. But some people eat reptiles. In the south of the U.S., some people eat snake meat. Alligator steaks are popular in the same area. In some parts of Australia, crocodile steaks are popular. Frog's legs are a French dish. People eat them in other places, too, like in the U.S., China and the Dominican Republic. Some people in Central and South America eat iguana meat.

Insects

Insects aren't a usual food, but many people like them. Some people in countries in Africa and in the Middle East eat grasshoppers. They're a snack in Mexico, and people can buy them at food markets in China. People also eat crickets and dragonflies in some parts of the world.

sushi

cricket soup

fried grasshoppers

snake meat

How adventurous are you?
Would you eat these foods?

2 Vocabulary

★ Food

a ▶ **CD1 T59** Look at the food in the pictures and write the words from the box in the blanks. Then listen, check, and repeat.

> tomatoes eggs bread strawberries
> cheese onions ~~chicken~~ apples bananas

MEAT

1   _chicken_

VEGETABLES

Peppers   5 ....   Cauliflower

Potatoes   6 ....   Carrots

Grocery Store

40

2 ....

3 ....

4 ....

OTHER GROCERIES

OPEN

FRUIT

7 ....

8 ....

9 ....

b Tell your partner which things you like and which you don't like.

A: *I like bananas.*

B: *Oh, I don't like them, but I love apples.*

3 Grammar

✱ Count and noncount nouns

a Look at the pictures on page 51, and then write the words from the box in the table.

> tomato ~~apple~~ egg bread ~~salt~~
> strawberry orange beef sugar
> onion ~~cheese~~ chicken ~~banana~~ rice

Count	Noncount
an apple	*some salt*
a banana	*some cheese*

b Look at the table in Exercise 3a and complete the rule.

> **RULE:** With singular count nouns, we use *a* or _____ .
> With noncount nouns, we use _____ . With plural count nouns, we use *some*.

✱ this/that/these/those

1 This is my water.

2 That is our bus.

3 These are your fries.

4 Those are her parents.

c Look at the pictures and complete the sentences with *this*, *that*, *these* and *those*.

1 _____ are his sandwiches.

2 Is _____ my bag?

3 _____ aren't her shoes.

4 I think _____ is your ice cream.

✱ I'd like ... / Would you like ... ?

d ▶ **CD1 T60** Listen to the dialogue. What does the man want to eat?

Woman: OK, let's have lunch. Would you like a salad?

Man: Yes, please. That's a good idea.

Woman: Would you like some cheese, tomatoes, lettuce and cucumber?

Man: Yes, please. And I'd like some potatoes if there are any.

Woman: Yes, there are! I have a lot of potatoes in the cupboard. And would you like some olives, too?

Man: No, thanks. I don't like olives!

Woman: OK, and then for dessert, some fruit. Would you like some strawberries and cherries?

Man: Yes, that sounds great!

e Write words in the blanks to make questions and answers.

1

A: Would you _____ a salad?

B: Yes, _____ .

2

_____ some cheese, tomatoes, lettuce and cucumber?

3

A: _____ some olives, too?

B: No, _____ .

4 Pronunciation

▶ **CD1 T61** Pronunciation section starts on page 114.

5 Listen and speak

a ▶ **CD1 T62** Look at the menu. Listen and check (✔) the things that the people order.

The Coach House
Dinner menu

APPETIZERS
Soup of the day
Goat's cheese with mushrooms
Tossed salad

MAIN COURSES
Chicken in lemon sauce
Baked salmon
Roast lamb
Vegetable curry

✱ All our main courses come with rice or potatoes.

DESSERTS
Fresh fruit salad
Ice cream (vanilla, chocolate and strawberry)

DRINKS
Fresh fruit juice
Tea
Coffee
Water

b Work in small groups. Role-play dialogues in a restaurant. Take turns being the waiter and the customer. Use the phrases in the box to help you.

Are you ready to order?
Would you like rice or potatoes?
What would you like to drink?

Enjoy your lunch!

6 Read and listen

a ▶ **CD1 T63** Look at the title of the story and the pictures. What food does Kate **not** like? Read, listen and check your answer.

1

Kate: Lunch! Great!

Izzie: Yeah. I'm really hungry. What do you have, Mark?

Mark: Lamb curry and rice. My mom's special recipe! Would you like some?

2

Izzie: Yes, please!

Mark: Kate?

Kate: No, thanks, Mark. I don't like lamb.

Mark: Oh, right. OK.

Darren: Mmm. This samosa is good!

Kate: Samosa? What's that, Darren?

Darren: Try one. Here you go!

Kate: Thanks!

3

Kate: Mmm. It's delicious! What's in it?

Darren: Well, some samosas have beef or vegetables, but this one has lamb!

Kate: You're joking! Lamb? Oh, now I feel silly!

Mark: Don't worry, Kate. Just enjoy your lunch!

4

b Read the story again. Put the sentences in the correct order.

a Darren says the samosa has lamb in it. ☐

b Kate says she doesn't like lamb. ☐

c They sit down to eat their lunches. ☐ *1*

d Kate feels silly. ☐

e Darren says he likes samosas. ☐

f Kate tries a samosa, and she likes it! ☐

7 Everyday English

a Find the expressions in the story. Who says them?

1 Yes, please. ....

2 No, thanks. ....

3 Oh, right. ....

4 Don't worry. ....

b How do you say each of the expressions in your language?

c ▶ CD1 T64 Read the dialogue and put the sentences in the correct order. Then listen and check.

☐ **Andy:** Yes, it's blue, but don't worry. It's really delicious!

6 **Andy:** Yes, please! I love fries!

☐ **Andy:** It's cheese. It's called Gorgonzola. Would you like some?

☐ **Samantha:** No, thanks. I don't like cheese very much. And that cheese is blue!

1 **Samantha:** What's that? In your sandwich.

☐ **Samantha:** Oh, right. But I think I'll just eat my fries. Do you want one?

d Fill each blank with one expression from Exercise 7a.

1 A: Jack, would you like some pizza?

  B: ...., Sandy. I don't like pizza very much.

2 A: Come on, Alex. It's 8:30. We're late!

  B: .... Sorry, Elena. OK, I'm ready now. Let's go!

3 A: Is the homework difficult, Jane? Do you want some help?

  B: ...., Mom. Help me with question three!

4 A: I really want a hamburger. But I don't have any money.

  B: ...., Mike. I have some money. I can buy some hamburgers.

8 Improvisation

Work in groups of four. Take two minutes to prepare a short role play. Try to use some of the expressions from Exercise 7a. Do not write the text, just agree on your ideas for a short scene. Then act it out.

Roles: Kate, Izzie, Mark and Darren

Situation: At school during lunch break

Basic idea: The four friends are hungry. They open their lunch boxes and tell each other what they have. They are not very happy. But then Darren has an idea: they can exchange lunches with each other.

9 Free Time ⊙ DVD Episode 4

a Who are they? Where are they? What are they doing? Write a short dialogue between the people in the photo.

b Check (✔) the statements that are true for you. Put an X to say "Not true for me."

1 I love potato chips. ☐

2 Goat's cheese and mushrooms – yuck! ☐

3 I really don't like fruit. ☐

4 Chicken is delicious. ☐

5 It's good to try new things. ☐

10 Write

a You are going to the United States next month to stay with an American family. Read the email from them. Where do they live? What do they want to know?

To: student16@aeim.cup
From: bs_johnson@aeim.cup

1 file(s) attached
johnsons.jpg **download**

Dear _____ ,

We're very happy you want to stay with us next month. We'd like to learn all about what you like before you arrive. Please write to us and tell us all about you! What food do you like? Is there any food you don't like? What's your favorite food?

Also, please tell us what you'd like to do here in Boston!

Best wishes and see you soon,

Adrian and Kerry Johnson

P.S. This is a photo of us with our dog, Ruff. Please send us a photo of you!

b Write your reply to the email. Start like this:

To: bs_johnson@aeim.com
From: student16@aeim.com

1 file(s) attached
me.jpg **attach file**

Dear Adrian and Kerry,

Thank you for your letter and the photo!

Here's a photo of my family and me.

11 Last but not least: more speaking

Work in groups of four.

a Each of you writes a list of four things to eat on a piece of paper. Make sure the others do not see what you are writing.

b Fold the lists, and put them in a bag or a box.

c Each of you takes out one of the lists. Unfold it, and read it.

d One of you starts. He/She talks about the food on the list, saying two sentences that are true and two sentences that are not true. The others listen.

e In the end, each of you says what you think is true/false.

Example:

I love tomatoes. I never eat lamb, I don't like it.
Carrots are my favorite vegetable.
My mom likes fruit salad.

> I think it isn't true that you like tomatoes. And I think it isn't true that your mom likes fruit salad.

Check your progress

1 Grammar

a Complete the sentences with *has / doesn't have / have / don't have.*

1 My mother __has__ brown hair. (+)

2 Jim and Ed are brothers, but they _____ the same color eyes. (−)

3 Sandra and Kate _____ five cousins. (+)

4 I _____ a new bicycle, but I hate it. (+)

5 I _____ any brothers. (−)

[4]

b Read the dialogue. Write the words from the box in the blanks.

> a   an   some

A: Hello, what would you like?

B: Hi. I'd like __a__ bag of rice and ¹_____ sugar, please.

A: Anything else?

B: Yes, and ²_____ eggs, please.

A: OK, that's six dollars, please.

B: Oh, and I'd like ³_____ apple and ⁴_____ banana, please.

[4]

c Match the questions and answers.

1 Why are chimpanzees and people similar?

2 Why don't you eat chocolate?

3 Why wouldn't you like a fighting cricket as a pet?

4 Why doesn't she like her hair?

5 Why do you want to work with dogs?

a Because I don't like sugar.

b Because it's wavy.

c Because I like animals.

d Because their DNA is 98% the same.

e Because they're noisy.

[4]

d Complete the sentences with words from the box.

> ~~this~~   that   these   those

1 I'd like __this__ apple.

2 I'd like _____ bananas.

3 I'd like _____ carrots.

4 I'd like _____ sandwich.

[3]

2 Vocabulary

Write the words from the box in three lists.

> arm   kangaroo   butter   chicken
> hamster   finger   sugar   ~~fish~~
> mouth   cat   ~~tomatoes~~   ~~foot~~

Parts of the body	Animals	Food
foot	_fish_	_tomatoes_

[9]

How did you do?

Check your score.

Total score	😊	😐	😞
[24]	Very good	OK	Not very good
Grammar	15 – 12	11 – 9	8 or less
Vocabulary	9 – 8	7 – 6	5 or less

9 I sometimes watch TV.

* Simple present with adverbs of frequency
* Vocabulary: days of the week, TV shows, telling the time

1 Read and listen

a Look at the pictures of Caleb and Mawar. What can you say about them? Put a check (✔) or an X in the correct places. Then read the article and check.

		Caleb	Mawar
1	lives on a very small island		
2	has a father who is a fisherman		
3	goes to school where he/she lives		
4	walks to school		
5	uses a computer at home		

b ▶ CD2 T02 Read the article again and listen. Answer the questions.

1 Where is Caleb from? Where is Mawar from?
2 Does Mawar watch TV at home? Why / Why not?
3 How does Caleb get to school?
4 What does Caleb's father do? What does his mother do?

Different places – different lives

Caleb

Caleb lives on Isle au Haut, an island in Maine in the U.S. The island is very small. It is ten kilometers long and three kilometers wide, and there are fewer than 100 people on the island.

Caleb's father is a fisherman. He often leaves the house before 6:00 a.m. His mom works at a small hotel. Caleb's sister goes to school on Isle au Haut. The students are 5 to 13 years old, and they all have one teacher. There are only seven students. Caleb is 15, and he goes to school on a bigger island. It often takes 45 minutes by boat to get to school!

Everyday things are not easy on Isle au Haut. For example, Caleb and his family sometimes use a computer at home to search the Internet and send emails, but there is hardly ever a good connection.

Mawar

Mawar lives in the village of Kertajaya in West Java in Indonesia. It is 80 kilometers to a city from Mawar's home. It's a seven-kilometer walk to a large school. But Mawar never goes to that school. There is a temporary school in Mawar's village, and that's where she and 100 other students have class every day. "I can't walk seven kilometers to school and back again every day. It's too far," Mawar says. "The school in our village is great. The building is old, but that's OK. I can always go to school, and I never have to walk far."

Having modern things is not common in Kertajaya. Mawar and her family don't have a computer or a TV at home.

2 Vocabulary

✱ Days of the week

▶ **CD2 T03** Listen and repeat.

Monday
Tuesday
Wednesday
Thursday
Friday
Saturday
Sunday

3 Grammar

✱ Adverbs of frequency

100%	always
	usually
	often
	sometimes
	hardly ever
0%	never

a Complete the sentences about Caleb and Mawar with the words in the box.

1 Caleb's dad __*often*__ leaves the house before six o'clock.

2 It _____ takes Caleb 45 minutes to get to school.

3 He _____ uses a computer at home.

4 There is _____ a good Internet connection.

5 Mawar _____ goes to the school that's seven kilometers away.

6 Mawar _____ watches TV at home.

b Complete the rule. Write *before* or *after* in the spaces.

RULE: Adverbs of frequency usually come _____ the verb *be*, but _____ other verbs.

c You can also talk about frequency like this.

every	day
	week
	morning
	month
	year

once		day
twice	a	week
three times		month
		year

d ▶ **CD2 T04** Complete the sentences with expressions from Exercise 3c. Then listen and check.

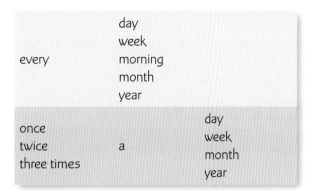

1 My mom checks her email at 8 a.m. and 8 p.m.

My mom checks her email twice a day.

2 Tom eats fruit on Mondays, Tuesdays, Wednesdays, Thursdays, Fridays, Saturdays and Sundays.

3 Susan goes shopping on Mondays, Wednesdays and Saturdays.

4 Harry plays soccer on Saturdays.

4 Speak

Work with a partner. Tell him/her about you and when you do things. Use the words in the box.

play soccer   go swimming   watch TV   go shopping
do homework   go to the movies   eat bananas
check email   wear black   .... (your ideas)

A: *I check my email once a day.*

B: *I don't. I only check my email two or three times a week.*

B: *I never eat bananas because I don't like them.*

A: *Really? I often eat bananas.*

5 Vocabulary

✱ TV shows

a How often do you watch TV? What channel do you usually watch? Are there interesting TV shows for teenagers in your country?

b ▶ **CD2 T05** Look at the pictures, listen and repeat the names. Then think of an example for each type of show from your country.

①
documentaries

②
soap operas

③
the news

④
sports programs

⑤
sitcoms

⑥
talk shows

⑦
game shows

⑧
cartoons

⑨
reality shows

6 Pronunciation

▶ **CD2 T06** Pronunciation section starts on page 114.

7 Listen and speak

a ▶ CD2 T07 Listen to the two dialogues. Complete the table with information about how often the two people watch TV.

How often?	Dialogue 1	Dialogue 2	Me	My partner
TV	*every day*	*a few shows a week*		
talk shows				
sports programs	*usually*			
movies				
the news				
soap operas				
reality shows				
game shows				
cartoons				
documentaries				

b What do you watch? Complete the *Me* column in Exercise 7a.

c Work with a partner. Ask and answer questions to complete the *My partner* column in Exercise 7a.

A: *Do you like talk shows?*
B: *Yes, I do.*
A: *How often do you watch them?*

8 Vocabulary

✱ *What time is it?*

a ▶ CD2 T08 Listen. Write the numbers in the boxes. Then listen again and repeat.

b ▶ CD2 T09 Listen to these times. Then listen again and repeat.

c ▶ CD2 T10 Listen to four conversations. Write the times you hear.

1 _____ 2 _____ 3 _____ 4 _____

9 Speak

a Look at the table. Write the times for you under *Me*.

b Work with a partner. Ask and answer questions and write the times under *My Partner*.

A: *What time do you usually get up in the morning?*
B: *At six thirty. What time do you get up?*
A: *I usually get up at seven o'clock.*

	Me	My partner
get up in the morning	*7:00*	*6:30*
have breakfast		
arrive at school		
have lunch		
do your homework		
have dinner		

10 Read and listen

a Look at the pictures of Carmen and Paul. What kinds of TV shows do you think they like?

b ▶ **CD2 T11** Read Carmen's profile and complete the information in the table in Exercise 10c.

What American teenagers watch

Carmen Woods

Carmen is 16. She lives in San Francisco, California. She doesn't watch TV every day. She's selective. She chooses which shows to watch. This is what she says about TV.

"No, I don't watch TV every day. I think it can be a waste of time. My favorite shows are competitions, like *America's Got Talent*. I always watch that. The people do great things. And that's why I like it a lot. I also watch documentaries, especially about life in other countries, because I really like geography. I sometimes watch cartoons on the weekend. I watch about eight hours of TV a week, I guess. I never watch sports programs. I don't like them at all. And I hardly ever watch the news."

c ▶ **CD2 T12** Now listen to Paul and complete the missing information in the table.

	age	show(s) he/she doesn't like	favorite shows	number of hours a week he/she watches TV
Carmen			*America's Got Talent*	
Paul				

Paul Evans

d ▶ **CD2 T12** Listen to the interview with Paul again. <u>Underline</u> the correct words.

1 Paul lives in *Northfield / <u>Southfield</u>*.
2 Some of Paul's favorite shows are *sitcoms / reality shows*.
3 Paul watches *soccer / basketball* on TV.
4 He usually watches *10 / 12* hours of TV each week.
5 Paul usually watches more TV *in the mornings / in the evenings*.

e Do you think that teenagers in your country are similar to Carmen and Paul, or different? Why?

11 Write

a There's a TV survey in your school magazine. Read Jason's paragraph about what shows he watches and how often.

I watch TV every weekend and sometimes after school. I like game shows, and my favorite show is *Cash Cab*. I like it because it's interesting and funny. I usually watch it once a week. I never watch soap operas because I think they're boring, and I don't like cartoons at all because my brother always watches them!

b Write a paragraph about the TV shows you like for your school magazine. Use Jason's paragraph to help you.

For your portfolio

10 Don't do that!

* Negative imperatives
* Vocabulary: adjectives to describe feelings

1 Listen

a Work with a partner. Look at the pictures. They tell a story.
Put the pictures in the order you think is correct.

b ▶ **CD2 T13** Now listen and check your ideas. Write 1–6 in the boxes.

2 Grammar

✳ Negative imperatives

a ▶ CD2 T13 Look at these sentences from the story on page 64. Who says them, Julie or Steve? Write *J* for Julie or *S* for Steve in the boxes. Then listen to the story again and check your answers.

1 Stay here. ☐   2 Don't go away. ☐

3 Come back! ☐   4 Don't do that. ☐

5 Don't go outside. ☐   6 Don't worry. ☐

b Complete the rule.

> **RULE:** Negative imperatives use .... + verb (base form without *to*).

c Look at the pictures. What are the people saying? Use the verbs from the box.

go away   laugh   touch it   cry   ~~shout~~   open

1 ....*Don't shout*............ !   2 .... !   3 .... !

4 .... the window!   5 .... !   6 .... !

d Match the two parts to make sentences 1–6, then match with signs A–F. Write 1–6 in the boxes.

1 Don't use ......   a this door.
2 Don't park ......   b this water.
3 Don't walk ......   c your cell phone.
4 Don't open ......   d the flash on your camera.
5 Don't drink ...... e your car here.
6 Don't use ......   f on the grass.

 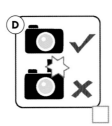  

Pronunciation

▶ **CD2 T14 and T15**

Pronunciation section starts on page 114.

4 Vocabulary

✽ Adjectives to describe feelings

a ▶ **CD2 T16** Write the words from the box under the pictures. Then listen, check and repeat.

> confused   scared
> ~~bored~~   worried   excited
> sad   happy   angry

b ▶ **CD2 T17** Listen to these six people. How do they feel?

1 _____angry_____
2 _____
3 _____
4 _____
5 _____
6 _____

5 Speak

Work with a partner. How do you feel?

1 You have a test tomorrow morning.

   A: *How do you feel?*
   B: *I'm worried!*

2 It's the first day of summer vacation.

3 You don't understand your English homework.

4 You hear strange noises late at night.

5 Your team is in the final game of a competition!

6 Your friend says something bad about you.

1 _____bored_____

2 _____

3 _____

4 _____

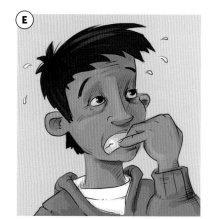

5 _____

6 _____

7 _____

8 _____

6 Read

a Read Julie's email. Does she still like Steve?

> To: Steven7@aeim.com
> From: julie.smith@aeim.com
>
> Dear Steve,
>
> I'm confused, and I'm very angry about yesterday. It isn't the first time, is it? I was really scared. Sometimes you're not very nice, and then I get angry.
>
> Your text message today says that you like me a lot. Well, sorry, but it's too late. I don't like you any more. Don't visit me again. Don't write and don't call.
>
> I have a new boyfriend, so leave me alone. It's all over for us.
>
> Goodbye,
>
> Julie

b Read the email again. Write *T* (true) or *F* (false).

1 Julie is angry and bored. [F]
2 Steve says he still likes her. [ ]
3 Julie doesn't like Steve. [ ]
4 Julie wants Steve to contact her. [ ]
5 Julie has another boyfriend now. [ ]

7 Listen

a ▶ CD2 T18 Listen to the song and read the words. Choose the best option.

1 The song says "Think about yesterday."
2 The song says "Think about today."
3 The song says "Think about tomorrow."

b Look at the underlined phrases in the song. Match them with the meanings a–f.

a tomorrow and the days after tomorrow [ ]
b not a long time [ ]
c I never wanted to hurt you [ ]
d you aren't happy in the morning [ ]
e I want you to be happy [ ]
f yesterday isn't here any more [ ]

c ▶ CD2 T18 Listen to the song again. Do you think it's a happy song or a sad song?

Don't stop
by Fleetwood Mac

If ¹you wake up and don't want to smile,
If it takes ²just a little while,
Open your eyes and look at the day,
You'll see things in a different way.

[*chorus*] Don't stop thinking about tomorrow,
Don't stop, it'll soon be here,
It'll be here, better than before,
³Yesterday's gone, yesterday's gone.

Why not think about ⁴times to come,
And not about the things that you've done?
If your life was bad to you,
Just think what tomorrow will do.
[*chorus*]

⁵All I want is to see you smile,
If it takes just a little while,
I know you don't believe that it's true,
⁶I never meant any harm to you.
[*chorus*]

Don't you look back.
Don't you look back.

Kate looks great!

8 Read and listen

a ▶ **CD2 T19** Look at the title of the story and the pictures. What does Izzie want to change about herself? Read, listen and check your answer.

1

Ray: Hi, Kate. What's wrong?

Kate: Hi, Ray. Nothing. Well, the thing is, I'm stressed about my homework.

2

Izzie: Wow! Kate's hair is great!

Ray: Don't worry about it, Kate. It's only homework! Anyway, I have work to do, too. Bye.

Kate: OK. See you, Ray.

3

Izzie: I hate my hair. I want to change it completely.

Jo: What for? Don't change it! I think you have nice hair!

Izzie: I don't know. I want hair like Kate's. Everybody thinks her hair's really nice.

4

Jo: Why do you want to be like Kate, Izzie? I think it's important to be yourself. People like you because you're YOU. Not because of your hair!

b Read the story again. Circle the correct answers: a or b.

1 What is Kate worried about?
   a Her homework.   b Her hair.

2 Who has work to do?
   a Jo.   b Ray.

3 What does Izzie want to change?
   a Her hair.   b Kate's hair.

4 Who does Izzie talk to about her hair?
   a Jo.   b Kate.

5 Why do people like Izzie?
   a Because she has nice hair.   b Because she's herself.

9 Everyday English

a Find the expressions in the story. Who says them?

1 What's wrong? ....
2 The thing is, ...
3 Anyway, ...
4 I think ... .

b How do you say each of the expressions in Exercise 9a in your language?

c ▶ CD2 T20 Read the dialogue and put the sentences in the correct order. Then listen and check.

☐ **Kevin:** I'm fine thanks, Polly. But what about you? I don't think you're very happy. What's wrong?

6 **Kevin:** Oh, you're right. It <u>is</u> late. Let's go!

☐ **Kevin:** Oh, that's sad. But don't worry. I'm sure she'll be OK.

1 **Polly:** Hi, Kevin. How are you?

☐ **Polly:** Nothing really. Well, the thing is, my cat's sick. She's old, too, and I'm worried about her.

☐ **Polly:** Yes, maybe. Anyway, let's go. I don't want to be late for school.

d Fill each blank with an expression from Exercise 9a.

1 **A:** Where's Tom?
   B: I'm not sure, but .... he's in his bedroom.

2 **A:** Hi, Joanna. Can I talk to you? I have a problem.
   B: Sure, Caroline. ....

3 **A:** Go on, Ben. Buy that shirt. It's great!
   B: No, it's very expensive, and .... , I don't really like it.

4 **A:** Why don't you want to come with me to the basketball game?
   B: Well, ... , I have lots of work to do, and anyway basketball is boring!

10 Improvisation

Work in pairs. Take two minutes to prepare a short role play. Try to use some of the expressions from Exercise 9a. Do not write the text, just agree on your ideas for a short scene. Then act it out.

Roles: Izzie and Jo

Situation: At the youth center

Basic idea: Izzie has a new hair style. Her hair looks like Kate's. Jo doesn't like this.

Start like this:

Izzie: Look, Jo. Do you like my new hair?

Jo: Do you really want to know?

11 Free Time

a Who are the people? Where are they? Write a short dialogue between the people in the photo.

b Work with a partner. Read the questions. Think of answers and make up a story of about 80 words. Write it on a piece of paper. Then read it aloud.

● Someone (Mark, Darren, Izzie or Kate) is babysitting. Who?
● He/She isn't happy about babysitting. Why (not)?
● Then something happens. What?
● In the end, another person has an idea. Who is it? What's the idea?

12 Write

a You get an email from an old friend. Who is new in her school? What questions does she ask?

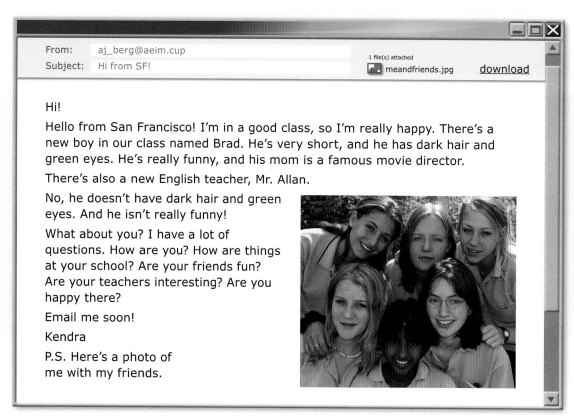

From: aj_berg@aeim.cup
Subject: Hi from SF!

1 file(s) attached
meandfriends.jpg   download

Hi!

Hello from San Francisco! I'm in a good class, so I'm really happy. There's a new boy in our class named Brad. He's very short, and he has dark hair and green eyes. He's really funny, and his mom is a famous movie director.

There's also a new English teacher, Mr. Allan.

No, he doesn't have dark hair and green eyes. And he isn't really funny!

What about you? I have a lot of questions. How are you? How are things at your school? Are your friends fun? Are your teachers interesting? Are you happy there?

Email me soon!

Kendra

P.S. Here's a photo of me with my friends.

b Write an email to your old friend about these things:

- your friends (hair, eyes, etc. / funny, nice, etc.)
- one thing you like about your school or teachers
- one thing you don't like

13 Last but not least: more speaking

✱ A game: Simon Says

Work in groups of four. One of you is the game master. You tell the others what (not) to do. They must be careful. When you say "Simon says …" they must do what you tell them. When you don't say "Simon says …" they must not do it. If they do, they get an X. A student who gets 3 Xs is "out" and cannot play anymore.

Example:

Simon says "Jump!"

Correct!

Touch your book.

Not correct – one X!

Remember: you can make things harder by using sentences that begin with "Don't …"!

For your portfolio

Check your progress

1 Grammar

a Complete the sentences with the correct form of the verbs in the box.

> ask   read   go   ~~watch~~   play   eat

1 My mom _watches_ the news on TV at nine.
2 Tom _____ swimming every weekend.
3 Paul _____ soccer with his cousin every Sunday.
4 We _____ fish on Fridays.
5 My friend _____ a lot of questions in our English classes.
6 My parents _____ three newspapers on Sundays!

| | 5 |

b Put the words in the correct order.

1 She / late / always / is
  She is always late.
2 chicken / We / usually / on Mondays / eat
  _____
3 on weekends / I / shopping / go / always
  _____
4 I / in the morning / tired / usually / am
  _____
5 at us / smiles / often / teacher / The
  _____
6 hardly / I / eat / ever / fruit
  _____

| | 5 |

c Underline the correct words.

1 The phone's ringing! *Don't answer / Answer* it for me, please!
2 Great to see you! *Don't come / Come* again!
3 *Don't watch / Watch* basketball tonight! I want to see a movie.
4 *Don't write / Write* to her soon! She misses you.
5 This food is awful. *Don't eat / Eat* it!

| | 4 |

2 Vocabulary

a Write the days of the week.

1 T _h_ _u_ _r_ _s_ _d_ _a_ _y_
2 S _ _ _ _ _ _
3 M _ _ _ _ _ _
4 W _ _ _ _ _ _ _ _
5 T _ _ _ _ _ _
6 S _ _ _ _ _ _ _
7 F _ _ _ _ _ _

| | 6 |

b Write the times.

 1 _12 o'clock_ _____

 2 _____

 3 _____

 4 _____

 5 _____

| | 4 |

c Underline the correct word.

1 I'm *excited / confused*. I don't understand this homework.
2 Don't shout at me! Why are you so *angry / bored*?
3 She's really *worried / excited*. It's her birthday today!
4 He's *scared / bored* because it's a really hard test.
5 She's crying. Why is she so *happy / unhappy*?

| | 4 |

How did you do?

Check your score.

Total score	☺ Very good	☺ OK	☹ Not very good
28			
Grammar	14 – 11	10 – 9	8 or less
Vocabulary	14 – 11	10 – 9	8 or less

11 Yes, I can!

* *can/can't* (ability)
* *like / don't like + -ing*
* Vocabulary: sports

1 Read and listen

a Look at the pictures. Who do you think the two men are? What sports event are they doing? Read the article and check your ideas.

"We never win, but we always win."

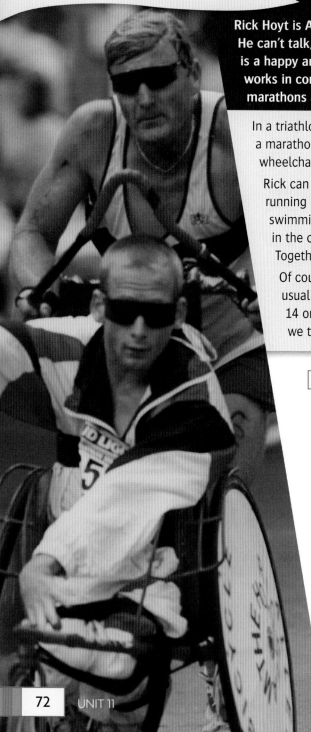

Rick Hoyt is American. He is in a wheelchair because he has cerebral palsy. He can't talk, so he uses a computer to communicate with people. Rick is a happy and successful man. He has a job at Boston College, and he works in computer studies. Rick loves sports too, and he participates in marathons and triathlons.

In a triathlon, people swim 4 kilometers, cycle 180 kilometers and then run a marathon, 42 kilometers. Rick can't run, cycle or swim because he's in a wheelchair. So how can he participate in a triathlon?

Rick can participate because he does it with his father, Dick Hoyt. In the running part of the event, his father pushes him in his wheelchair. In the swimming, Rick lies in a small boat and Dick swims and pulls him. And in the cycling, Rick sits in a special seat on the front of Dick's bike. Together, they are "Team Hoyt."

Of course, Team Hoyt never wins the race. The winner of a triathlon usually finishes in about nine hours. The Hoyts usually take about 14 or 15 hours. "That's right," says Dick. "Rick and I never win. But we think that we always win."

b ▶ **CD2 T21** Read the article again and listen. Answer the questions.

1 How does Rick talk to people?
2 What do people do in a triathlon?
3 How does Dick help Rick in a triathlon event?
4 What name do Rick and Dick have when they do a triathlon?
5 How long do they take to finish a triathlon?
6 Dick says: "We think that we always win." Why do you think he says that?

> **Did you know ...?**
> Team Hoyt's best marathon time is 2 hours and 40 minutes. (The best runners in the world usually run a marathon in about 2 hours and 5 minutes.)

2 Grammar

✳ *can/can't* (ability)

a Look at the examples. How do you say these sentences in your language?

*Rick **can't** talk.*

*How **can** Rick participate in a triathlon?*

b Look at the text on page 72 again. <u>Underline</u> other examples with *can* or *can't*.

c Complete the table.

Affirmative	Negative	Question	Short answer
I/you/we/they/he/she/it **can** swim.	I/you/we/they/he/she/it .... **(cannot)** swim.	.... I/you/we/they/he/she/it swim?	Yes, I/you/we/they/he/she/it **can**. No, I/you/we/they/he/she/it .... **(cannot)**.

d Make sentences.

1 John + read German / − write it

   John can read German, but he can't write it.

2 Claire + ride a bike / − swim

   Claire ....

   ....

3 Chimpanzees + learn to count / − learn to speak English

   Chimpanzees ....

   ....

4 I + use a computer / − draw pictures with it

   I ....

   ....

5 She + play the guitar / − play the violin

   She ....

   ....

6 My sister + play the piano / − sing

   My sister ....

   ....

7 Uncle Jim + fly a plane / − ride a bike

   Uncle Jim ....

   ....

8 My mom + sing / − play the guitar

   My mom ....

   ....

3 Listen

▶ **CD2 T22** Listen and write *T* (true) or *F* (false).

1 Camels can live without water for 16 months. ☐

2 People can see 1 million different colors. ☐

3 Kangaroos can hop 100 meters. ☐

4 A man from the U.S. can eat 94 worms in 30 seconds. ☐

5 A Cuban man can go 162 meters under water without oxygen. ☐

4 Pronunciation

▶ **CD2 T23 and T24**

Pronunciation section starts on page 114.

5 Speak

Work with a partner. Ask and answer questions using the words in the box. Add two more questions.

A: *Can you swim?*

B: *Yes, I can, but not very well. Can you play the piano?*

A: *No, I can't.*

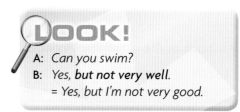
| swim | play the piano | juggle | walk on your hands | use a computer | sing |

6 Vocabulary

✱ Sports

▶ **CD2 T25** Match the words from the box with the pictures. Write the words in the spaces. Then listen, check and repeat.

play tennis
ride a horse
skate
play basketball
do gymnastics
cycle
snowboard
ski
play soccer
skateboard
play (American) football
~~play volleyball~~

1 *play volleyball* 2 _____ 3 _____

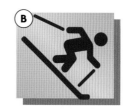

4 _____ 5 _____ 6 _____

7 _____ 8 _____ 9 _____

10 _____ 11 _____ 12 _____

7 Listen

a ▶ CD2 T26 Hannah is from New York City and Sam is from England. Listen to their conversation about sports. Check (✔) the sports they talk about.

1 volleyball ☐
2 (American) football ☐
3 swimming ☐
4 tennis ☐
5 basketball ☐
6 soccer (football) ☐
7 rollerblading ☐
8 gymnastics ☐

b ▶ CD2 T26 Listen again. Write *T* (true) or *F* (false).

1 Hannah goes roller-blading every day. ☐
2 Sam likes playing tennis, but he doesn't like watching it on TV. ☐
3 Hannah likes watching (American) football games. ☐
4 Sam plays soccer on his school team. ☐

8 Grammar

✳ *like / don't like + -ing*

a Look at the examples and the table. Then complete the rule.

I like watching tennis on TV.
I don't like playing it.
I love going to the games.

Affirmative	Negative	Question	Short answer
I really **like** swimming. I **love** watching tennis on TV. I **hate** playing soccer.	I **don't like** cycling.	**Do** you **like** playing games?	Yes, I do. No, I don't.

RULE: When you talk about activities, use the *-ing* form of the verb, after the verbs _____ , _____ and _____ .

b Put the words in the correct order.

1 like / tennis / We / playing / don't
We don't like playing tennis.

2 going / the / like / to / movies / She / doesn't
----

3 like / your / Do / on / going / parents / vacation?
----

4 really / soccer / brother / likes / watching / His
----

5 swimming / hate / in / I / ocean / the
----

c Complete the questions. Put the verbs in parentheses in the correct form.

1 Do you like _____ sports on TV? (watch)
2 Do you _____ sports every weekend? (watch)
3 Do you _____ early on the weekend? (get up)
4 Do you like _____ early? (get up)
5 Do you _____ to the movies a lot? (go)
6 Do you like _____ to the movies? (go)

9 Speak

a Work with a partner. Ask each other the questions in Exercise 8c. Write down his/her answers.

b Work with another partner. Tell him/her about your first partner's answers.

Claudia likes swimming, but she doesn't like watching sports on TV. She gets up early every day, but ...

Culture in mind

10 Read and listen

a Match the names of the sports with the photos. Write 1–6 in the boxes.

1 swimming
2 volleyball
3 wrestling
4 track and field
5 gymnastics
6 tennis

b Read about Shannon and Doug. Write their names under the photos of the sports they play.

c ▶ **CD2 T27** Read the article again and listen. Complete the sentences with *Shannon* or *Doug*.

1 .... likes volleyball.
2 ....'s favorite sport is track and field.
3 .... can do gymnastics.
4 .... likes a sport where you run.
5 .... loves tennis.
6 .... likes competing as a team.

d Look at the "Did you know?" box, and answer the questions.

1 What sport is popular because it's not expensive?
2 When do teenagers usually play soccer?

A

B

C

D

Not only baseball, basketball and football

Teenagers in the U.S. can play a lot of sports at school. Baseball, basketball and football are very popular, but there are other things teens can do!

Shannon Harris is 16, and she's a junior (11th grade) at a high school in Detroit, Michigan. "Volleyball and swimming are cool," she says. "But I love gymnastics. You have to compete as individuals and as a team. I love working together as a group."

Doug Thomson is 17, and he's a senior (12th grade) at the same high school. He loves playing tennis, and he likes wrestling. But his favorite sport is track and field. "There are so many different things I can do in track and field," he says. "It's not just running. I can do the high jump, the discus throw and the pole vault, too."

E ....

F ....

Did you know?

- Many American high schools don't have soccer teams, but many teenagers play on soccer teams after school.

- Basketball is a popular sport with teens because it's not expensive. You only need a basketball and a net.

- Baseball is the oldest team sport in the U.S., and it's still popular with teens today.

- In high schools, there are separate teams for girls and boys in most sports.

- For some sports, such as football and wrestling, high schools only have boys' teams. A girl can sometimes play on the boys' teams for these sports.

11 Write

a Read this email from Jon. Who's his favorite tennis player?

From: jonkhan@aeim.cup
Subject: my favorite sports

Hi .....

Thanks for your email! I really like reading about your family and friends.

At school, we have new tennis courts and a new football field. In the U.S., most people love football. I don't like football because I can't play it well. I love playing tennis, and I think I'm pretty good at it. I like watching it on TV, too. My favorite player is Andy Roddick.

Do you like sports? Please write and tell me about the sports you play in your country and the sports you like and don't like.

Your friend,

Jon

b Write your reply to Jon's email.
Write about:

- popular sports in your country
- sports you do at school
- sports you like / sports you don't like
- your favorite athlete

For your portfolio

12 A bad storm's coming.

* Present continuous
* Vocabulary: house and furniture

1 Read and listen

a Read the text quickly. What's the man's job? What's he doing this year?

AROUND THE WORLD – ALONE

John White is a bus driver. He likes his job, but he *loves* his boat. Once a year, John goes on a short trip in the boat. His wife Pauline and son Andy often go with him.

This year is different. John is taking a year off from his job and is sailing around the world. And he's doing it alone. An exciting journey? Yes and no. "Sometimes, dolphins and whales swim along with the boat, and sometimes I sail past beautiful tropical islands," says John. "But sometimes the weather gets bad, and then I have problems." John wants to …

b ▶ CD2 T28 Read the text again and listen. Write *T* (true) or *F* (false).

1 John sails around the world every year.   [F]

2 John is sailing around the world now.   [ ]

3 Pauline is with him on his boat.   [ ]

4 Everything on his journey is good.   [ ]

2 Listen

a ▶ CD2 T29 Here is a telephone conversation between John and Pauline. Complete the dialogue with the words from the box. Then listen and check.

> it's starting   They're swimming
> are you doing   I'm eating
> I'm getting   He's taking

Pauline: Hi, John. How are you?

John: Fine, yeah, I'm fine. How are you? What ¹_____?

Pauline: Oh, ²_____ breakfast in the kitchen. Andy's upstairs in the bathroom. ³_____ a shower. So, are you OK?

John: Yes, I'm making good progress. And ⁴_____ very close to South Africa.

Pauline: Great!

John: Yes, and guess what? I can see dolphins outside! ⁵_____ next to the boat.

Pauline: Oh, how nice!

John: It is! But I'm worried. The weather's getting bad. There's a strong wind now, and ⁶_____ to rain. A bad storm's coming, I think. Sorry Pauline, I can't talk any more. I have to go outside.

Pauline: John? Can you hear me, John?

b Match the beginnings and endings of the sentences.

1 John is   ......   a swimming.

2 Pauline is   ......   b getting bad.

3 Andy is   ......   c looking out of the window.

4 The dolphins are   ......   d taking a shower.

5 The weather is   ......   e eating breakfast.

3 Grammar

✳ Present continuous

a Look at the examples. <u>Underline</u> other examples of the present continuous in the conversation on page 78. Then complete the rule and the table.

*I'm **making** good progress.*
*The weather's **getting** bad.*

Affirmative	Negative	Question	Short answer
I'm (am) working.	I'm not work_____ .	_____ I work_____ ?	Yes, I _____ . No, I _____ .
You/we/they _____ (are) work**ing**.	You/we/they _____ (are not) work_____ .	_____ you/we/ they work_____ ?	Yes, you/we/they _____ . No, you/we/they _____ .
He/she/(it) _____ (is) work**ing**.	He/she/(it) _____ (is not) work_____ .	_____ he/she/(it) work_____ ?	Yes, he/she _____ . No, he/she _____ .

> **LOOK!**
> Spelling
> have – having
> make – making
> shop – shopping

> **RULE:** We use the _____ to talk about things that are happening now. We use the present tense of the verb _____ + the -*ing* form of the main verb.

b Complete the sentences with the present continuous form of the verbs.

1 **A:** Can I talk to Caroline?
  B: No, sorry. She's in her bedroom. She ___*'s writing*___ a letter. (write)

2 **A:** Mom, where's Dad?
  B: He's in the bathroom. He _____ a shower. (take)

3 **A:** Where's Dan?
  B: He's in the park. He _____ soccer with his friends. (play)

4 **A:** Can you help me?
  B: Not right now. I _____ my lunch. (have)

5 **A:** Where are you?
  B: I'm in a bookstore in town. I _____ my sister a book. (buy)

c Make questions and answers with the present continuous.

1 he / go to school?/ no / come home
  Is he going to school? No, he isn't. He's coming home.

2 they / eat ice creams? / no / drink milkshakes
  _____
  _____

3 she / read a book? / no / listen to music
  _____
  _____

4 your father / work today? / no / take a day off
  _____
  _____

4 Listen

▶ CD2 T30 Listen to six sounds. What are the people doing?

1 She *'s brushing her teeth.*

2 He _____ .

3 They _____ .

4 She _____ .

5 He _____ .

6 They _____ .

5 Speak and write

a Look at the pictures and write sentences about the people. Then work with a partner and read your sentences aloud.

Katie's reading and listening to music.

Katie

Daisy

Ben and Liz

Max

Tom and Amy

Sam

b Work with a partner. Cover your sentences and ask and answer questions about the people in the pictures.

A: *Is Katie playing soccer?*

B: *No, she isn't, she's reading. Are Ben and Liz ... ?*

c Work with a partner. Say where your friends and family are now and what they are doing.

A: *My brother's at work. I think he's working on his computer.*

B: *My mom and dad are going to work, and my sister's at school. I think she's studying math now.*

6 Pronunciation

▶ CD2 T31 Pronunciation section starts on page 114.

7 Vocabulary

✳ House and furniture

▶ **CD2 T32** Match the words in the boxes with the numbers and letters in the picture. Write the letters and numbers next to the words. Then listen, check and repeat.

kitchen _1_	yard _____	stairs _____
living room _____	bathroom _____	
bedroom _____	garage _____	

door _____	sofa _____	armchair _____
stove _____	chairs _____	window _a_
refrigerator (fridge) _____	table _____	bed _____
bathtub _____	shower _____	toilet _____

8 Speak

Work with a partner. Talk about your house or apartment.

There's a fridge and a stove in the kitchen.
The TV's on a table in the living room. We don't have a garage.

LOOK!

Prepositions

in   on   under

Just five minutes!

9 Read and listen

a ▶ **CD2 T33** Look at the title of the story and the pictures. What does Darren want to do? Read, listen and check your answer.

1

Darren: Hi, Izzie.

Izzie: Hey, Darren. What's up?

Darren: Nothing. But I'm bored. How about a little bit of soccer?

Izzie: Sorry, Darren. Not now. I'm working.

2

Darren: Mark, my friend!

Mark: Hey, Darren. What are you doing?

Darren: Looking for someone to play ... soccer!

Mark: Sorry. I'm busy. I'm finishing this. Why don't you ask Ray?

3

4

Ray: I don't know, Darren. I have a lot of things to do.

Darren: Oh, Ray. Just five minutes!

Ray: Oh, all right, then. Five minutes – no more!

Ray: Goal! Goal! Team Ray 1, Team Darren 0! Yes!

Darren: Oh, no! Let's stop, Ray. I'm tired!

Ray: Come on, Darren, another five minutes! OK?

b Read the story again. Answer the questions.

1 What's Izzie doing in picture 1?
2 What's Mark doing in picture 2?
3 What's Ray doing in picture 3?
4 In picture 4, why does Darren want to stop playing soccer?

10 Everyday English

a Find these expressions in the story. Who says them?

1 ... a little bit of ... .
2 Why don't you ... ? ....
3 ... a lot of ... .
4 ... all right ... .

b How do you say each of the expressions in Exercise 10a in your language?

c ▶ CD2 T34 Read the dialogue and put the sentences in the correct order. Then listen and check.

☐ **Millie:** Oh, all right, Dad. Maybe you're right.

☐ **Millie:** Dad? I'm going out now, OK? *(marked 1)*

☐ **Millie:** But I'm almost finished, Dad. I can finish tomorrow morning. I have a little time before my English class.

☐ **Dad:** Well, Millie, why don't you finish it now? Then you can go out and have fun, and not worry about it any more.

☐ **Dad:** I know! *(marked 6)*

☐ **Dad:** What? But Millie, you have a lot of homework.

d Fill each blank with an expression from Exercise 10a.

1 **A:** I feel really tired every morning.
   B: Well, ... go to bed at 11 o'clock and not 12 o'clock?

2 **A:** Why don't we go to the movies tonight?
   B: Oh, ... Let's go and see the new Leonardo DiCaprio movie.

3 **A:** Adam? Can I have .... your ice cream?
   B: No, you can't! Go and buy your own ice cream!

4 **A:** Do you like Eric?
   B: No, not really. .... people think he's nice, but I don't like him.

11 Improvisation

Work in groups of four. Take two minutes to prepare a short role play. Try to use some of the expressions from Exercise 10a. Do not write the text, just agree on your ideas for a short scene. Then act it out.

Roles: Darren, Mark, Izzie and Ray.

Situation: At the youth center.

Basic idea: Ray needs help from the kids, but whatever he says, they find an excuse ("Sorry, I'm studying English!" "Sorry, I'm ..."). Ray asks them again and again, but they always find different excuses. In the end, Ray has an idea ...

12 Free Time ⊙ DVD Episode 6

a It is someone's birthday. Who? What are the others doing?

b There is a surprise. What is it?

c Write answers to complete these sentences:

- three things you can do on a friend's birthday are ...
- three things you usually do on your birthday are ...
- three things you would like to do on your birthday are ...
- three things that you would not want to do on your birthday are ...

13 Write

a Lucy is on vacation in Portugal with her family. Read her postcard to Alex, and then answer the questions.

1 Where is the hotel?
2 Why does Lucy like the hotel?
3 Where are Lucy's parents?
4 What is Lucy doing?
5 What's the weather like?

Dear Alex,

Here I am in Portugal! I'm having a great time. The weather's fantastic - really sunny and warm. We're staying in a small hotel near the beach. The hotel has a swimming pool - great! My parents aren't here right now. They're shopping in town. So I'm here alone, and I'm having breakfast - in the sun! Hope you're OK. See you soon.

Love,

Lucy

Alex Campbell
336 Elm Road
Princeton, NJ
08540
USA

b You are on vacation with your family. Write a postcard to your English-speaking friend. Use Lucy's postcard and the questions to help you.

● Where's the hotel?
● What are you doing?
● What's the weather like?

LOOK!

What's the weather like?

It's raining. It's cloudy. It's sunny.

14 Last but not least: more speaking

a Work in pairs. Imagine you are on vacation somewhere. Take two minutes to answer the following questions. Make notes of your answers:

● Where are you?
● What are you doing right now? (sitting in a café? eating ice cream? skiing? swimming?)
● Who is with you?
● What are you enjoying about your vacation?
● What are you not enjoying?

b Sit back to back with your partner. Make a phone call to each other and ask and answer questions about your vacations.

A: Hi, ... ! Where are you?
B: Oh, hi ... ! I'm on vacation right now.
A: Really? Where are you!
B: I'm in ...
A: What are you doing?
B: I'm ...

Check your progress

1 Grammar

a Write the words in the correct order.

1 don't / playing / like / I / tennis
I don't like playing tennis.

2 on / soap operas / watching / you / Do / TV / like
....

3 My / swimming / ocean / in / brother / likes / the
....

4 cat / Her / milk / doesn't / drinking / like
....

[ ] 3

b Write sentences about what the people can and can't do.

1 I _can juggle_ (+ juggle), but I _can't swim_ (– swim).

2 My dad .... (+ stand on his head), and he .... (+ walk on his hands).

3 Tessa .... (+ do gymnastics), but she .... (– rollerblade).

4 Kylie and Annie .... (– sing), but they .... (+ dance).

[ ] 6

c Complete the dialogues. Use the present continuous.

1 A: Hi, Liz. What _are_ you _doing_? (do)
  B: I .... (read a book)

2 A: Can I talk to Claudia, please?
  B: No, sorry. She .... (take a shower)

3 A: Are Peter and Angela here?
  B: Yes. They're in the living room. They .... (watch TV)

4 A: Where's Rick?
  B: He's in Emma's room. He .... (look for his phone)

5 A: Which girl is Caroline?
  B: That's her, over there. See? She .... with Jack. (dance)

[ ] 5

2 Vocabulary

a Put the letters in order and write the names of the sports.

1 entsin ...._tennis_.........
2 lovelblyal ....
3 roosdbawn ....
4 kbodatsrea ....
5 askalbetbl ....
6 clngiyc ....
7 ynagsmstic ....

[ ] 6

b Write the names of rooms and furniture in a house.

1 _k i t c h e n_
2 r _ _ _ _ g _ _ _ t _ _
3 _ _ _ i _ g   _ o _ m
4 t _ _ l e
5 b a _ _ r _ _ _
6 _ h _ w _ _
7 _ _ f _
8 _ e _ _ _ _ m
9 _ o _ _ e _

[ ] 8

How did you do?

Check your score.

Total score	☺	☺	☹
[ ] 28	Very good	OK	Not very good
Grammar	14 – 11	10 – 9	8 or less
Vocabulary	14 – 11	10 – 9	8 or less

13 Special days

* *can/can't* (asking for permission)
* Prepositions: *at, in, on*
* *one/ones*
* Vocabulary: months of the year and seasons, clothes

1 Read and listen

a Look at the photos. Say what you can see in each one.

b Read the article and match the photos with the special days. Write 1–3 in the boxes.

Inverness
Aberdeen
SCOTLAND
Edinburgh
Glasgow

Scotland – a land of traditions

Scotland has lots of beautiful places to visit, and there are some special days there, too. Here are three of them.

1 Burns Night

Every year on January 25, the Scots remember a famous poet named Robert Burns. Usually there is a special dinner, and people eat haggis (which is made from different parts of a sheep). People play music, and they read Burns's poems aloud.

2 Hogmanay

Hogmanay is an important holiday for the Scottish people. It is on December 31 – New Year's Eve. Like everywhere in the world, Scottish people celebrate the New Year with a party. Then, early in the morning on January 1, they put on warm coats and go "first footing." They visit the homes of their friends and take a piece of bread and a piece of coal to bring their friends food and warmth all year.

3 Highland Games

In the summer, there are Highland Games days all over Scotland. The men wear socks and kilts, a type of skirt with a special pattern called "tartan." Women wear beautiful skirts, blouses and scarves. There is dancing, and the bands play music. There are a lot of athletic events, too. A famous one is "tossing the caber." Men try to throw a six-meter tree trunk (the "caber").

January

c ▶ **CD2 T35** Read the article again and listen. Write the names of the special days.

1 People go to friends' houses ....

2 People eat special food ....

3 People dance and do athletic events ....

2 Vocabulary

✳ Months of the year and seasons

a ▶ **CD2 T36** Listen and underline the syllables with the main stress. Then listen, check and repeat.

January

February

March

April

May

June

July

August

September

October

November

December

b Find examples of the months in the text on page 86 and underline them.

c ▶ **CD2 T37** Match the names of the seasons with the photographs. Write 1–4 in the boxes. Then listen, check and repeat.

1 summer   2 winter   3 spring   4 fall

d Which season goes with which months in your country? What's your favorite season? Why?

3 Grammar and speaking

✳ Prepositions: *at, in, on*

a Study the examples in the table.

at	in	on
seven o'clock	June	Monday
9:30	March	Tuesday
	the summer	
	the winter	

b Complete the sentences with the words from the box.

on   in   at

1   The movie starts .... 8:30 tonight.
2   I have English class .... Monday, Wednesday and Friday.
3   My mother's birthday is .... June.
4   We usually go to my grandparents' house .... the spring.

c Work with a partner. Tell each other true things about you. Use the prepositions from the box in Exercise 3b.

My birthday is in June.
My best friend's birthday is in April.
I usually get up at 7:30, but on Sunday I get up at 10:00.
I always go to the movies on Saturdays.

4 Vocabulary

✱ Clothes

a ▶ **CD2 T38** Match the names of the clothes with the picture. Write 1–12 in the boxes. Then listen, check and repeat.

> 1 ~~T-shirt~~   2 scarf   3 shirt   4 dress   5 pants   6 sweater   7 socks   8 jacket   9 top
> 10 jeans   11 shoes   12 sneakers

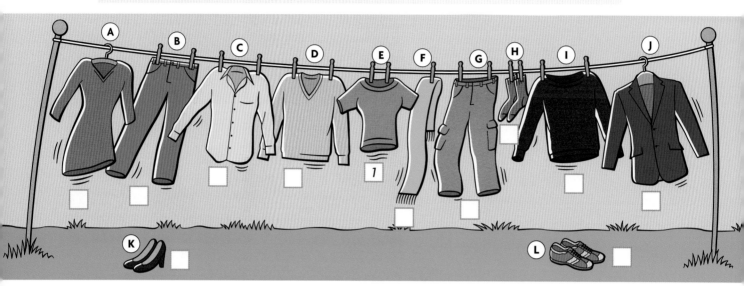

b Read the text in Exercise 1 on page 86 again. (Circle) all the words for clothes.

5 Listen

▶ **CD2 T39** Listen and number the pictures 1–4.

6 Speak

a Work with a partner. Find a picture of a person in this book. Say what the person is wearing, but don't say the person's name! Can your partner find the same picture?

A: *She's wearing ...*

B: *It's ... on page ...*

b Work with a partner. Ask and answer the questions. Write down your partner's answers.

- How often do you go shopping for clothes?
- What kinds of clothes do you like?
- Do you like shopping for clothes? Why / Why not?
- What are your favorite stores?
- Do you like shopping alone or with your friends?

7 Pronunciation

▶ **CD2 T40 and T41** Pronunciation section starts on page 114.

8 Grammar

✱ *can/can't* (asking for permission)

a Read the two dialogues. What do the people want to buy?

1

Man: Hi. You have some sneakers in the window. Can I try them on?

Assistant: The black ones? Yes, of course you can. What size?

Man: Size 10.

Assistant: OK. Just a moment.

2

Woman: Hello. Can I have that green shirt, please?

Assistant: What size?

Woman: Um, large I think.

Assistant: Sorry, we don't have the green one in large.

Woman: OK. Can I try on a medium?

b Look at the example. When do we use *Can I ... ?*

Can I try them on?

c <u>Underline</u> other examples of *Can I ...?* in the dialogues in Exercise 8a.

d ▶ CD2 T42 Listen to the dialogues and number the pictures 1–4.

e ▶ CD2 T43 Listen to two of the dialogues again and write the missing words in the blanks. Then listen again and repeat.

1 **Boy:** _____ I use your MP3 player?

  Girl: No, sorry Jake, _____ . I'm using it.

  Boy: OK.

2 **Girl:** Is that magazine good?

  Boy: Yes, it's great.

  Girl: _____ I read it?

  Boy: Yes, of course you _____ ! Here you are!

f Work with a partner. Use the pictures to make conversations.

✱ *one/ones*

g Look at these examples from the dialogues in Exercise 8a. When do we use *one* and *ones*?

You have some sneakers in the window.
*The black **ones**? (**ones** = sneakers)*

Can I have that green shirt, please?
*Sorry, we don't have the green **one**. (**one** = shirt)*

h Write *one* or *ones* in the blanks to replace the words that are crossed out.

1 **A:** I like those pants in the window.

  B: Which ~~pants~~ _____ones_____ ?

  A: The black ~~pants~~ _____ , over there, in the corner.

2 **A:** Can I see the shirt in the window, please?

  B: Sorry, which ~~shirt~~ _____ ? The green ~~shirt~~ _____ ?

  A: No, the red ~~shirt~~ _____ .

Culture in mind

9 Read and listen

a Look at the pictures and the title of the article. Then read the sentences and write *T* (true) or *F* (false). Say what you think! Read the article and check your ideas.

1 Edinburgh is the capital of Scotland.
2 There is a festival in Edinburgh every four years.
3 The Edinburgh Festival is only about music.
4 Only people from Scotland perform at the festival.
5 There is a famous music-and-dancing event at night in the castle.

The Edinburgh Festival

Every summer there is a big festival in Edinburgh, the capital city of Scotland. Do you love dancing? Laughing? Movies? Plays? Well, the Edinburgh Festival is the place for you. There's something for everyone!

The "Edinburgh International Festival" started in 1947. Artists and actors come from around the world, and there are many exhibitions and performances.

People talk about "The Edinburgh Festival," but there are really several festivals that all happen in August. There is a film festival, a theater festival, a jazz festival, a book festival and many others.

A famous event is the Edinburgh Tattoo. Army bands from Scotland and other countries play music inside Edinburgh Castle at night. There is dancing, too, especially Scottish country dancing. Every year, over 200,000 people watch the Tattoo and listen to the famous Scottish bagpipes.

People come from all over the world to see the events in Edinburgh. Hotels and guest houses are always full, so if you want to see the festival, it's important to plan early. Do you want to go? Start planning now!

b ▶ **CD2 T44** Read the text again and listen. Answer the questions.

1 When did the Edinburgh Festival start?
2 Is the Edinburgh Festival just one event, or is it many events?
3 What happens at the Edinburgh Tattoo?
4 How many people go to the Tattoo each year?
5 Why is it important to plan a trip in advance for the Edinburgh Festival?

c Are there any festivals in your country? What can you say about them?

10 Write

a Read this email from Steve in the U.S. What do people do during Mardi Gras?

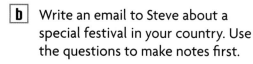

| From: | Steve_Harris@aeim.cup |
| Subject: | Mardi Gras |

Dear ...,

Every year in February or March, there is a huge celebration in New Orleans called Mardi Gras. People enjoy music, dancing and parades. Mardi Gras lasts for two weeks! There is music in the streets, people wear colorful clothes and they sing and dance all day and all night. People hear many types of music during Mardi Gras. New Orleans is famous for its jazz music and Zydeco.

People wear costumes in parades and on the street. Every year, one man is the king of the carnival. He wears purple, green and gold clothes. Other people wear colorful clothes and masks. During Mardi Gras, many people eat typical New Orleans food, such as gumbo (a thick soup) and beignets (a fried pastry).

Do you celebrate Mardi Gras in your country? Do you have other festivals with special clothes and food? Can you write and tell me about one? I'd love to know what you do there!

Write soon,

Steve

b Write an email to Steve about a special festival in your country. Use the questions to make notes first.

- What's the festival called?
- When is it?
- What do people do? (music, clothes, food, parades)

Use your notes and Steve's email to help you.

* Simple past: *was/wasn't; were/weren't*
* Vocabulary: time expressions, ordinal numbers and dates

1 Read and listen

a Look at the photographs and the title of the article. What do you think the text is about? Who were the three men? Read the article quickly and check your ideas.

The history of pop

This week:

Buddy Holly and the Day the Music Died

On February 3, 1959, three men were in a small plane over Iowa in the U.S., at one o'clock in the morning. They were Buddy Holly, Richie Valens and J. P. Richardson (or The Big Bopper).

The three men were singers and musicians. Buddy Holly was very successful, with hit songs like "Peggy Sue" and "That'll Be the Day." Valens and The Big Bopper were stars, too.

It was a very cold night, and there was snow and a lot of wind. The plane wasn't in the air for very long when there was a problem. The plane went down and crashed. The three musicians and the pilot were all dead.

Buddy Holly was only 22, and Richie Valens was only 17. The Big Bopper was 28.

In 1971, another singer, Don McLean, wrote a song about that terrible day. It was called "American Pie" and was about "the day the music died."

Next week: The Beatles' last concert

b ▶ **CD2 T45** Read the text again and listen. Write *T* (true) or *F* (false).

1 The men were in a small car.   *F*
2 Buddy Holly's real name was J. P. Richardson.
3 The plane was in the air for a long time.
4 Four men died in the crash.
5 Buddy Holly had a hit called "American Pie."

② Grammar

✱ Simple past: *was/wasn't; were/weren't*

a Look at these examples from the article on page 92 and complete the table.

*Three men **were** in a small plane.*
*Buddy Holly **was** only 22.*
*The plane **wasn't** in the air for very long.*

Affirmative	Negative	Question	Short answer
I/he/she/it _____ late yesterday.	I/he/she/it **wasn't** late yesterday.	Was I/he/she/it late yesterday?	Yes, I/he/she **was**. No, I/he/she _____.
We/you/they **were** late yesterday.	We/you/they _____ (**were not**) late yesterday.	_____ we/you/they late yesterday?	Yes, we/you/they **were**. No, we/you/they **weren't**.

b <u>Underline</u> other examples of sentences with the simple past of the verb *be* on page 92.

c Circle the correct options.

1 I was / were at home yesterday evening.
2 My brother *was / were* at home, too.
3 There *was / were* a soccer game on TV, the U.S. and England.
4 The American players *wasn't / weren't* very good.
5 My brother and I *wasn't / weren't* happy.
6 But our mother isn't American. She's from England, so she *was / were* happy!

d Complete the questions with *Was* or *Were*.

1 __*Were*__ the three men in New York?
2 _____ they on a bus?
3 _____ the three men stars?
4 _____ it a warm night?
5 _____ there a problem with the plane?
6 _____ the three singers dead?
7 _____ Buddy Holly 25 years old?

③ Pronunciation

▶ **CD2 T46 and T47** Pronunciation section starts on page 114.

④ Vocabulary and speaking

✱ Time expressions

a Write the words from the box in the blanks in the table.

evening   afternoon   month   weekend

Last	night	Yesterday	morning
	week		_____
	_____		
	_____		

b Look at the table. Think about yesterday. Write where you were at the different times.

	Me	My partner
6 a.m.	*in bed*	
9 a.m.		
1:30 p.m.		
5 p.m.		
8 p.m.		
11:30 p.m.		

c Work with a partner. Ask and answer questions about yesterday. Use the times in the table and the expressions in Exercise 4a. Write your partner's answers.

A: *Where were you at six o'clock yesterday morning?*
B: *I was in bed. What about you?*
A: *Me, too.*
B: *Where were you at ... ?*

d Tell the class about your partner's day.

Marcia was in bed at six o'clock yesterday morning. She was with her friends last night at 8:00.

UNIT 14   93

(5) Read and listen

a Read the text quickly and then answer the questions.

1　Which pop group is the text about?

2　Why was this concert important?

A rooftop concert

On January 30, 1969, people on a street in London were surprised. There was music coming from the roof of an office building. It was live music, and it was the Beatles! They played five songs. It was a free concert, and all the songs were new.

The Beatles weren't very happy together, and it was their last concert. In 1970, they stopped playing as a group.

b What do you know about the Beatles? Answer the questions.

1　Where were the Beatles from?

2　How many men were there in the group?

3　What were their names?

c ▶ CD2 T48 Tom talks to his grandmother about the Beatles. Listen and check your answers.

Liverpool

London

d ▶ CD2 T48 Listen again and write *T* (true) or *F* (false).

1　The Beatles were his grandmother's favorite group. ☐

2　You never hear Beatles songs on the radio now. ☐

3　"Miss You" was a famous Beatles song. ☐

4　The Beatles were still together in 1969. ☐

5　John Lennon was 50 when he died. ☐

6 Vocabulary

✳ Ordinal numbers and dates

a ▶ CD2 T49 Listen and repeat.

1st (first)	2nd (second)
3rd (third)	4th (fourth)
5th (fifth)	6th (sixth)
7th (seventh)	8th (eighth)
9th (ninth)	10th (tenth)
12th (twelfth)	13th (thirteenth)
20th (twentieth)	30th (thirtieth)

b ▶ CD2 T50 Listen and write the numbers.

1 _3rd_   2 ....
3 ....   4 ....
5 ....   6 ....
7 ....   8 ....

c Work with a partner. Ask and answer questions.

A: *What's the first month?*
B: *January. What's the seventh month?*

d ▶ CD2 T51 Listen to four conversations and check (✔) the dates you hear.

1 December 5 ☐   December 6 ☐
2 June 13 ☐   June 30 ☐
3 January 4 ☐   January 14 ☐
4 April 21 ☐   April 23 ☐

e How do you say these dates?

12/27/1968 = December twenty-seventh, nineteen sixty-eight

f Work with a partner. Ask and answer the questions. Write your partner's answers.

1 When's your birthday?
2 When's your teacher's birthday?
3 When's your neighbor's birthday?
4 When's your best friend's birthday?

LOOK!

We write: *(On) December 8, 1980* or *12/08/1980.*
We say: *(On) December eighth, nineteen eighty* or
(On) December the eighth, nineteen eighty.

1 12/27/1968
2 11/30/1978
3 01/16/1985
4 10/17/1974
5 02/02/2003
6 03/01/1999

An accident in the park

7 Read and listen

a ► **CD2 T52** Look at the title of the story and the pictures. How did Izzie hurt her head? Read, listen and check your answer.

> **Izzie:** Hi, you two. Do you like my new hat?
> **Mark:** Poor you!
> **Kate:** Izzie, what happened?

Izzie: Well, this morning I was in the park, you know, skateboarding...

... and suddenly, there was a boy on a bike. A minute later, I was on the ground. My head hurt and the boy was gone!

> **Mark:** So it was the boy's fault. How awful!
> **Izzie:** No, Mark. It was *my* fault, not his. My helmet was on my arm, not on my head!
> **Kate:** Well, anyway, who was the boy? We have to find him.

b Read the story again. Look at the sentences. Find one thing that is wrong in each sentence and correct it.

1 This morning, Izzie was in the park, running.
2 There was a boy on a skateboard.
3 Izzie was on the ground, and her leg hurt.
4 Izzie's helmet was on her head.
5 Izzie thinks it was the boy's fault.
6 Mark wants to find the boy.

8 Everyday English

a Find these expressions in the story. Who says them?

1   Poor [you]!   ....

2   ... you know ...   .

3   ... suddenly ...   .

4   [It was] my fault   ....

b How do you say each of the expressions in Exercise 8a in your language?

c ▶ CD2 T53 Read the dialogue and put the sentences in the correct order. Then listen and check.

☐6☐ **Dave:** I know. But I feel terrible now. Poor Jenny. She's only seven!

☐ **Dave:** Well, I opened the door of our living room. She was on the floor, you know, playing with her toys. The door hit her arm. It was awful! And it was my fault!

☐ **Dave:** No, I'm not. My little sister's in the hospital. Her arm's broken.

☐ **Liz:** Oh, Dave, come on. It's not really your fault, you know. Accidents happen – especially at home.

☐1☐ **Liz:** Hey, Dave. Are you OK?

☐ **Liz:** Oh, no! Poor Jenny! What happened?

d Fill each blank with an expression from Exercise 8a.

1   A: Julia was strange last night.

    B: I know. At first, everything was fine. Then .... , she was really angry with me!

2   A: Look! My MP3 player's broken.

    B: I know. It's .... I'm really sorry.

3   A: Alan's at home today. He has a terrible cold.

    B: Oh, no. .... Alan! I hope he's OK soon.

4   A: Where are you going?

    B: To Steve's house, ... , to play computer games.

9 Improvisation

Work in groups of four. Take two minutes to prepare a short role play. Try to use some of the expressions from Exercise 8a. Do not write the text, just agree on your ideas for a short scene. Then act it out.

Roles: Darren, Mark, Izzie, Kate

Situation: In the youth center

Basic idea: One of the four has a broken laptop. The others ask what happened. The person with the laptop tells the story ... the laptop was on a chair, a little sister (or brother) was in the room, and ....

10 Free Time ⊙ DVD Episode 7

A stepladder

Paint

A tray of drinks

A cardboard box

a Work in pairs or small groups. Look at the four pictures. For each thing, imagine a possible accident. Mime your accidents.

b Think how the accidents could happen here. Now watch Episode 7.

11 Write

a Read the email from Jay to Maggie. Where was Jay on vacation? Was it a good vacation?

To: maggie.buxton@aeim.cup
From: jayadams@aeim.cup

1 file(s) attached
hotelpool.jpg   download

Hi, Maggie!

We were on vacation in Argentina last month, and it was wonderful! The weather was fantastic. It was sunny every day. There was a swimming pool at the hotel, and there was a great beach, too.

The food in the hotel wasn't very good, but there were lots of good cafés and restaurants downtown.

I hope we go there again next year!

Love,

Jay

b Write an email to a friend about a vacation. Use these questions and Jay's email to help you.

● when?   last year / summer / month

● weather?   not good / OK / wonderful

● swimming pool or beach?   great / not very nice

● hotel or restaurants?   good food / not very good food

12 Last but not least: more speaking

✳ When I was very young ...

a Talk to someone in your family and try to find out as much as you can about when you were very young. Use the questions to help you. Also, try to get a photo of you as a very young child.

● What was your first word as a baby?

● How big were you when you were born? (I was ... kilos.)

● Where was your first school?

● Who were your first friends?

● Who was your first teacher?

● What was your favorite food as a six-year-old?

● What food didn't you like?

● What was your favorite TV show when you were 10?

b In groups, show your photos. Then ask and answer questions.

Check your progress

1 Grammar

a Complete the sentences with the verbs from the box and *Can*.

> borrow ~~close~~ open play try on

1 I'm cold! __Can__ I __close__ the door, please?
2 .... my son .... this shirt, please?
3 It's so hot in here. .... we .... the window, please?
4 .... they .... their new CD now? It's really good!
5 Jack, you have two pencils. .... I .... one, please?

[5]

b Complete the sentences with *in*, *on* or *at*.

1 The store opens __at__ nine o'clock.
2 We never go to school .... Saturday.
3 My grandmother is coming to see us .... the weekend.
4 They like going skiing .... the winter.

[3]

c Complete the dialogue with the past simple form of *be*.

A: You __weren't__ at school last week. Where [1] .... you?
B: I [2] .... at home, in bed.
A: Oh, what [3] .... the matter with you? [4] .... you tired?
B: No, I [5] .... sick. My parents [6] .... worried.
A: I'm sure they [7] .... ! Well, our classes [8] .... very interesting.
B: Oh, good.

[8]

2 Vocabulary

a Write the words in the lists.

> June summer ~~spring~~ August ~~December~~ winter fall April

Months	Seasons
December	_spring_
....	....
....	....
....	....

[6]

b Put the letters in order to find six more clothes.

1 hitrs   __shirt__
2 antps   ....
3 sserd   ....
4 estrawe   ....
5 ocssk   ....
6 raneksse   ....
7 ajkect   ....

[6]

c Match the dates with the numbers.

1 September seventeenth, nineteen fifty-one   a 11/14/2003
2 August nineteenth, nineteen ninety-eight   b 02/03/1999
3 February third, nineteen ninety-nine   c 05/02/2006
4 November fourteenth, two thousand and three   d 9/17/1951
5 May second, two thousand and six   e 08/19/1998

[4]

How did you do?

Check your score.

Total score	🙂 Very good	😐 OK	🙁 Not very good
[32]			
Grammar	16 – 13	12 – 10	9 or less
Vocabulary	16 – 13	12 – 10	9 or less

15 What happened?

* Simple past: regular and irregular verbs; questions and negatives
* Vocabulary: verb and noun pairs

MISSISSIPPI ALABAMA GEORGIA

FLORIDA

1 Read and listen

a Look at the photos and the title of the article. What is the story about? Read the text quickly and check your ideas.

SHE SAID "NO"

On December 1, 1955, Rosa Parks left work in Alabama, in the U.S., got on a bus and sat down. More people got on the bus, and soon it was full. One man didn't have a seat. The bus driver said to Rosa: "Stand up! Give this man your seat!"

Rosa was tired after a long day at work. So, she quietly said: "No." This started something that changed the United States forever. Because Rosa Parks was a 42-year-old black woman and the man on the bus was white.

When Rosa was a young girl, she walked to school, but the white children took a bus. Rosa saw their bus every day when it went by. "In those days," she said, "there was a white world and a black world. I lived in the black world." She went to a black school and studied with black children.

When Rosa said "No," she broke the law. The law said a black person had to give his or her seat to a white person. The police came and took her to prison. Many black people in Alabama were very angry, and they stopped using the buses for a year. Then the law changed, and slowly, things started to change all over the U.S.

For the rest of her life, Rosa worked to help black people in the U.S. She died on October 25, 2005, at the age of 92.

b ▶ CD2 T54 Read the text again and listen. Answer the questions.

1 Why did the bus driver say to Rosa, "Stand up!"?
2 Why did Rosa say, "No"?
3 What was Rosa's world when she was a young girl?
4 Why did the police take Rosa to prison?
5 Why did black people stop using the buses in Alabama?

2 Grammar

✳ Simple past: regular verbs

a Look at the examples from the text on page 100. Then complete the rule.

*She **started** something that changed the U.S.*
*"I **lived** in the black world."*
*She **studied** with black children.*
*They **stopped** using the buses.*

> **RULE:** To form the simple past of most regular verbs, add _____. If the verb ends in _____, only add -d. If the verb ends in -y, change y to _____ and add -ed. If the verb ends in a vowel + one consonant, double the consonant and add _____.

b Read the text. Complete the sentences with the simple past form of the verbs in the box.

> like ~~watch~~ ask want start like
> die listen study

I _watched_ a good movie on TV last night. It was about the war in Korea in about 1952. In the war, an American soldier named Tom Granger almost [1]_____. A Korean soldier, Mun-hee Park, saved his life. Park's daughter, Jin, was a nurse. She took care of Tom, and she [2]_____ him a lot. Tom really [3]_____ Jin, too. But there was a problem: the language. Jin didn't speak English, and Tom didn't speak Korean. Tom really [4]_____ to understand Jin, so he [5]_____ to learn Korean. He [6]_____ to Jin a lot, he [7]_____ Korean grammar and he [8]_____ her a lot of questions. And after three years, his Korean was very good. Tom and Jin were very happy.

3 Pronunciation

▶ **CD2 T55 and T56** Pronunciation section starts on page 114.

4 Grammar

✳ Simple past: irregular verbs

a Look at these examples. <u>Underline</u> other simple past irregular verbs in the article on page 100. Then complete the table. Use the irregular verb list on page 117 to help you.

*She **left** work, **got** on a bus and **sat** down.*
*The police **came** and **took** her to prison.*

be	_was, were_
break	_broke_
come	_____
get	_____
go	_____
have	_____
leave	_____
say	_____
see	_____
sit	_____
take	_____

b Complete the sentences with the correct forms of the verb.

1 I _____wrote_____ a thank-you letter to my aunt yesterday. (write)

2 I _____ my friend Charlie at the party last night. (see)

3 The train to Scotland is slow, so we _____ by plane. (go)

4 I _____ a new bike from my parents for my birthday! (get)

5 I _____ to Sally yesterday. (speak)

c Put the verbs in the box in the simple past. Then complete the text about J.D. Salinger.

> be have know think write get become

Jerome David Salinger ____was____ born in New Hampshire in the U.S. in 1919. He [1]_____ many short stories, and in 1951, he [2]_____ famous for his book *Catcher in the Rye*. The book is still popular today.

J. D. Salinger [3]_____ married in 1955 and [4]_____ two children. He didn't like being famous. Many people [5]_____ he'd write many more books, but he stopped writing in 1965. No one [6]_____ why. Salinger died in 2010. He was 91 years old.

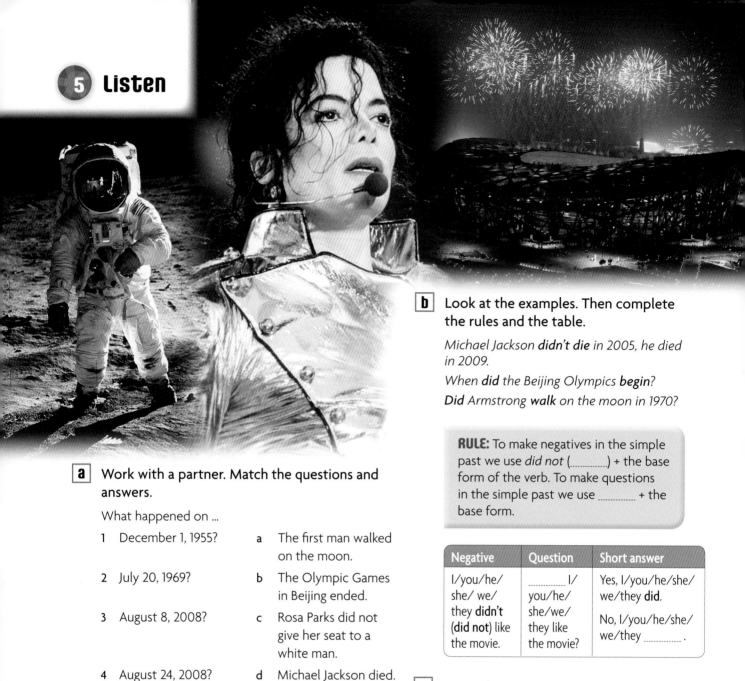

5 Listen

a Work with a partner. Match the questions and answers.

What happened on ...

1 December 1, 1955?
2 July 20, 1969?
3 August 8, 2008?
4 August 24, 2008?
5 June 25, 2009?

a The first man walked on the moon.
b The Olympic Games in Beijing ended.
c Rosa Parks did not give her seat to a white man.
d Michael Jackson died.
e The Olympic Games in Beijing started.

b ▶ **CD2 T57** Listen to a radio quiz show. Check your answers to Exercise 5a.

6 Grammar

✱ Simple past: questions and negatives

a Here are three things that the people on the quiz show said. Some words are missing. Write the words from the box in the blanks.

> walk   did   die   didn't   did   walk

1 When .... Michael Jackson .... ?
2 When .... the first man .... on the moon?
3 Neil Armstrong .... on the moon in 1979. It was 1969.

b Look at the examples. Then complete the rules and the table.

*Michael Jackson **didn't die** in 2005, he died in 2009.*

*When **did** the Beijing Olympics **begin**?*

***Did** Armstrong **walk** on the moon in 1970?*

> **RULE:** To make negatives in the simple past we use *did not* (............) + the base form of the verb. To make questions in the simple past we use .... + the base form.

Negative	Question	Short answer
I/you/he/ she/ we/ they **didn't** (**did not**) like the movie.	.... I/ you/he/ she/we/ they like the movie?	Yes, I/you/he/she/ we/they **did**. No, I/you/he/she/ we/they ....

c Write the negative sentences.

1 I arrived late. I *didn't arrive* late.
2 You used my computer. You .... my computer.
3 We watched the movie. We ....
4 She saw a lot of interesting things. She ....
5 They got a new computer. They ....

d Write the questions.

1 She watched the soap opera. What *did she watch* ?
2 It happened in New York. Where .... ?
3 They studied Chinese. What .... ?
4 I had a pizza on Saturday. When .... ?
5 We went to Brazil. Where .... ?

7 Speak

a Complete the questionnaire. Put a check (✔) for yes or an X for no in the *Me* column.

	Me	My partner
1 This morning, did you		
a take a shower?	☐	☐
b have coffee for breakfast?	☐	☐
c go to school by car?	☐	☐
2 Last night, did you		
a watch TV?	☐	☐
b go to bed before 11 o'clock?	☐	☐
c study?	☐	☐
3 Last weekend, did you		
a help your parents?	☐	☐
b go to the movies?	☐	☐
c play any sports?	☐	☐
4 Yesterday, did you		
a have ice cream?	☐	☐
b listen to music?	☐	☐
c practice English?	☐	☐

b Work with a partner. Ask and answer the questions from Exercise 7a and fill in the *My partner* column.

A: *Did you take a shower this morning?*

B: *Yes, I did. Did you?*

c Work with a partner. Use question words *what*, *when* and *where* to ask and answer questions.

A: *What did you do last night?*

B: *I studied English.*

A: *Did you? I watched a movie on TV. Where did you ... ?*

8 Vocabulary

✶ Verb and noun pairs

a Match the verbs and the nouns. Write the nouns in four lists. Use the questionnaire in Exercise 7a to help you.

> bed   ~~coffee~~   ice cream   school   sports
> the movies   English

have	practice	play	go to
coffee			

b Now add these nouns to the four lists in Exercise 8a.

> the piano (x2)   work   breakfast/lunch/dinner (x2)
> a party (x2)

9 Read and listen

a Look at the photos. What do you think the women did? Read the article and check your ideas.

The mother of TV

Yoo-hoo, Mrs. Goldberg!

Gertrude Berg played Molly Goldberg on a popular TV show over 50 years ago, but she did so much more ...

Gertrude was born in 1898 in New York City. Her father had a summer resort in the Catskill Mountains outside of the city. People came to the resort in the summers. Gertrude wrote plays for the children so they had something to do when it was raining outside. This is where her career in acting and writing started.

Gertrude wrote *The Goldbergs*, which was a radio show from 1929 to 1946. It became a television show in 1949. It was the first American sitcom, and it was on TV until 1956. It was about a family living in New York City. Molly Goldberg was the main character. Molly's neighbors yelled out their windows, "Yoo-hoo, Mrs. Goldberg!" When Molly came to the window, they all talked about their problems.

Gertrude was the star of the show, and she was the brains behind the show,

Gertrude Berg as Molly Goldberg

too. The idea for the show was hers, she wrote almost every episode, she hired the other actors and she was the director! Not many people know about Gertrude Berg, but she made it possible for many women, like Lucille Ball, to be on TV. She also invented the sitcom, an idea that many other TV shows are based on today.

Gertrude Berg

Lucille Ball

b ▶ CD2 T58 Read the article again and listen. Write *T* (true) or *F* (false).

1 Gertrude was born in the Catskill Mountains. ☐
2 Gertrude's father wrote *The Goldbergs*. ☐
3 *The Goldbergs* was a TV show for 20 years. ☐
4 *The Goldbergs* was about a family in New York City. ☐
5 It was the first American sitcom. ☐

6 Gertrude was an actress, a writer and a director. ☐
7 Lucille Ball was Molly Goldberg on TV. ☐
8 Everyone knows who Gertrude Berg is. ☐

10 Write

a Read this article from a school magazine.

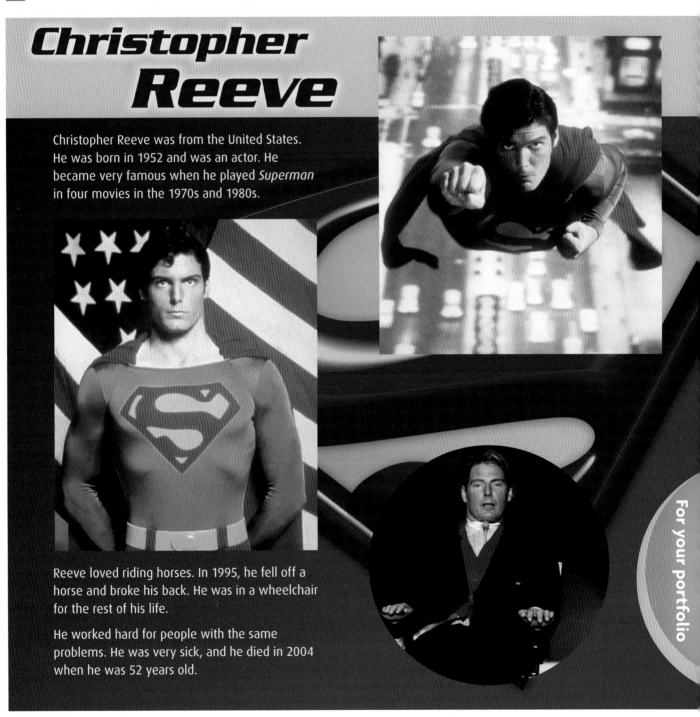

Christopher Reeve

Christopher Reeve was from the United States. He was born in 1952 and was an actor. He became very famous when he played *Superman* in four movies in the 1970s and 1980s.

Reeve loved riding horses. In 1995, he fell off a horse and broke his back. He was in a wheelchair for the rest of his life.

He worked hard for people with the same problems. He was very sick, and he died in 2004 when he was 52 years old.

For your portfolio

b Write a paragraph about a famous person from the past for your school magazine. Use the texts about Gertrude Berg and Christopher Reeve to help you.

16 Things change.

* Comparative adjectives
* *than*
* Vocabulary: adjectives and opposites

1 Listen

a Look at the photographs. What things are different and what things are the same?

Is life better now?

b ▶ CD3 T02 Listen to Dave and his grandmother. They talk about life in the 1960s and life now. Who talks about these things? Write *D* (Dave) or *G* (grandmother).

1 The streets in a town ☐
2 School life ☐
3 DVDs ☐
4 The stores ☐
5 Television ☐
6 Cell phones ☐

c ▶ CD3 T02 Listen again. Write *T* (true) or *F* (false).

1 Dave's grandmother thinks life is better now than in the 1960s. ☐

2 She didn't watch television when she was young. ☐

3 She thinks Dave's life at school is easy. ☐

4 Dave says it's easy for his grandmother to walk on the streets. ☐

5 Dave says his grandmother is a happy woman. ☐

2 Grammar

✱ Comparative adjectives

a ▶ **CD3 T02** Who said these sentences in the conversation? Write *G* (grandmother) or *D* (Dave) in the boxes. Then listen again and check your answers.

1 Life was great when I was a teenager. ☐
2 Now she's older. ☐
3 Some things are easier now. ☐
4 School life is more difficult now. ☐
5 People were friendlier in the '60s. ☐
6 Life is more interesting now. ☐
7 Is it better now? ☐
8 Maybe life is worse for her now. ☐

b Complete the table and the rule. Use the sentences in Exercise 2a to help you.

Adjective	Comparative adjective
old	*older*
big	bigger
young	
easy	*easier*
happy	
difficult	_____ difficult
interesting	_____ interesting
good	
bad	

RULE: Short adjectives: we usually add *-er*. If the adjective ends in *y*, change the *y* to _____ . If it ends in a vowel + consonant, double the consonant (e.g., *big → bigger*). Longer adjectives: add the word _____ before the adjective. Irregular adjectives: use a different word: good – *better*; bad – _____ .

c Write the comparative adjectives.

1 close _____
2 tall _____
3 cheap _____
4 funny _____
5 important _____
6 fast _____
7 expensive _____
8 hot _____

d Complete the sentences. Use the correct forms of the adjectives.

1 Rio's __*hot*__ , but Delhi's __*hotter*__ . (hot)
2 Trains are _____ , but planes are _____ . (fast)
3 Mike's joke was _____ , but Annie's joke was _____ . (funny)
4 Haytown's _____ , but Moreton's _____ . (close)
5 The Grand Hotel's very _____ , but the Plaza Hotel's _____ . (expensive)
6 Matt's really _____ , but Andy's even _____ ! (tall)

✱ than

e Look at the examples below on page 106.

*I was **freer than** him.*
*Life is **faster than** in the 1960s.*

f Rewrite the sentences in Exercise 2d.

*Delhi's **hotter than** Rio.*

3 Pronunciation

▶ **CD3 T03** Pronunciation section starts on page 114.

4 Speak

Compare some things and people in your classroom.

I'm older than Juan. Sandra's taller than Lisa.

My desk's closer to the door than Mandy's desk.

5 Read

a Look at the photos and the newspaper article. What does the man do? Where is he from? Read the article and check your ideas.

From London bank to Thailand hotel

Harley Smith is 28, and he is from London. He left school when he was 17 and went to work for a bank in London. He worked long hours, did well and made a lot of money. And now ... he's the owner of a small hotel on the island of Koh Tao in Thailand.

"I opened my hotel six months ago," says Harley. "There are six bedrooms here and a small restaurant, and I do almost everything. It's seven days a week here!"

So, why did he go there? "Well," he says, "life in London was great. You know, it's a very modern and exciting city. But it's noisy and very busy, and sometimes it's a little dangerous, too. And three years ago, I came here to Koh Tao on a scuba diving vacation, and I fell in love with the island. So, here I am! It's safer, it's quieter and it's more relaxing."

Does he miss London? "No, not really," says Harley. "Well,

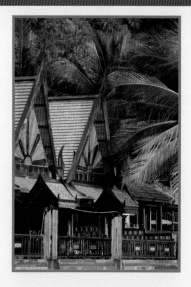

sometimes! It's great here, but London's my hometown. I was born there, and I have friends there, too. I miss them sometimes. But the thing is, life here is much better. I go to bed at night, and the only thing I hear is the ocean. It's wonderful!"

b Answer the questions.

1 What was Harley's first job?

2 What does his hotel have?

3 Is the hotel hard work for Harley? How do you know?

4 When did Harley first go to Koh Tao?

5 What does Harley miss about London?

6 What does Harley like in Koh Tao at night?

6 Vocabulary

✳ Adjectives and opposites

a Look at the sentences from the article on page 108. Which one is about Koh Tao?

1 It's a very modern and exciting city.

2 It's noisy and very busy.

3 It's safer, it's quieter and it's more relaxing.

b ▶ **CD3 T04** Write the words from the box under the pictures. Then listen and check.

> ~~dangerous~~ boring exciting modern
> noisy old-fashioned quiet safe

1

a _dangerous_ street

2

a _____ place

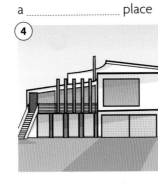

3

a _____ club

4

a _____ house

5

an _____ car

6

a _____ game

7

an _____ movie

8

a _____ garden

c Put the words in Exercise 6b in pairs with their opposites. Write the words in the blanks.

1 exciting _____

2 dangerous _____

3 noisy _____

4 modern _____

7 Speak

a Work with a partner. Talk about things in your life. Use the adjectives in Exercise 6.

A: *Our house is modern, but I like old-fashioned houses.*

B: *Really? I like modern houses.*

A: *Our town is boring. There aren't any ...*

b Work with a partner. Use the topics in the box to make comparisons.

A: *Snowboarding is a dangerous sport.*

B: *That's true, but skiing is more dangerous than snowboarding.*

> a sport
> a movie
> a school subject
> a place in your town
> a text in this book
> a television show
> a city in your country
> a type of transportation (car, train, etc.)

So sorry.

8 Read and listen

a ▶ **CD3 T05** Look at the title of the story and the pictures. Is Izzie angry with Darren? Read, listen and check your answer.

Mark: Hey, Darren. What's the matter?

Darren: Hi, Mark. I feel awful. You see … this morning I was on my bike in the park, and I was in a hurry …

Darren: And there was a girl, skateboarding. I think she fell over, but I didn't stop. And now I feel terrible. You know, maybe she …

Mark: Don't worry, Darren. She hurt her head a bit, but she's all right.

Darren: What do you mean? How do you know?

Mark: Well, I know who the girl was! It was Izzie!

Darren: Izzie! I don't believe it!

Darren: I'm so sorry about what happened, Izzie. I had no idea it was you.

Izzie: That's OK, Darren. It was sort of my fault, really. Next time I go skateboarding, I'm going to put my helmet on my *head*!

Darren: Thanks, Izzie.

Izzie: That's OK, Darren! But you can buy me ice cream!!

b Read the story again. Mark the statements *T* (true) or *F* (false).

1 Darren doesn't feel good. ☐
2 The girl fell over and Darren stopped. ☐
3 Darren is surprised when Mark says the girl was Izzie. ☐
4 Darren says "sorry" to Izzie. ☐
5 Izzie is angry with Darren. ☐
6 Izzie wants Mark to buy her ice cream. ☐

9 Everyday English

a Find these expressions in the story. Who says them?

1 What's the matter ....
2 You see, ...
3 I don't believe it ....
4 ... sort of ... .

b How do you say each of the expressions in Exercise 9a in your language?

c ▶ CD3 T06 Read the dialogue and put the sentences in the correct order. Then listen and check.

☐ Phil: Oh, no. What's the matter? Not good news?

7 Phil: Well, you see, he studied really hard this year. How about you, Maggie?

☐ Phil: Hi, Maggie. Did you see the exam results? They came out today.

☐ Phil: Oh, French? You know, Tom Black got a 93 in French.

☐ Maggie: No. I'm sort of unhappy. I only got an 80 in French. I wanted a 90.

☐ Maggie: What? I don't believe it! He was always terrible at French.

☐ Maggie: Yes, I saw them unfortunately.

d Fill each blank with an expression from Exercise 9a.

1 A: Come and have pizza with us.
   B: Um, well, no thanks. ...., I'm not hungry, and I don't really like pizza anyway.

2 A: Paul, can I talk to you for a minute?
   B: Of course, Carrie. Wow, you look unhappy. .... ?

3 A: Did you buy the computer we saw last weekend?
   B: No, I didn't. It was nice, but it was .... expensive.

4 A: My brother Sam's going to college next year.
   B: .... ! College? But he was always terrible at school.

10 Improvisation

Work in pairs. Take two minutes to prepare a short role play. Try to use some of the expressions from Exercise 9a. Do not write the text, just agree on your ideas for a short scene. Then act it out.

Roles: Mark and Izzie

Situation: At school

Basic idea: Mark is unhappy. Izzie talks to him. Mark tells her about something bad that happened to him yesterday (for example, he heard that his grandmother was sick). Izzie thinks of something nice to do to help Mark to forget his problem.

11 Free Time ⊙ DVD Episode 8

a Who are the people? Where are they? Write a short dialogue between the people in the photo.

b Work in small groups. Imagine you are going to have an event at your school. The idea is to raise money to help poor or sick people. Write down 4–5 things that you (the people in your group) could do for visitors to have fun.

c Tell your ideas to other groups.

12 Write

a Look at the advertisement for a competition. How much money can you win? How many words do you have to write?

COMPETITION

Do you want the chance to **win $1,000** for your school?

Enter our competition!

Either: A Write a short text to compare your life now to your life six years ago.

Or: **B** Write a short text to compare life as it was 100 years ago to life as it is now.

Don't write more than 120 words!

b Read Claudia's entry. Which option did she write about, A or B?

I think my life is better now. I have more friends than I had six years ago. And I'm older, so I can do more interesting things. I can go to the movies, I can go out with friends and I can go to bed later in the evenings. I have my own room now and lots of DVDs and books. Six years ago, I didn't have my own phone or a laptop.

What are the things about my life now that I don't like? Well, I have more things to do at home and at school. School is more difficult, and I think my life is busier.

c Write your entry for the competition. Choose option A or B. Use Claudia's model to help you organize your answer.

13 Last but not least: more speaking

Life now and life 50 years ago: which is better?

Work in small groups.

a Imagine life 50 years ago in your country. Make a list of some differences between now and then (5–10 things).

b Look at the things you have written down. Which things do you think are better now? Which things do you think were better 50 years ago?

c Prepare to make a presentation of your ideas to your class. Look again at what you did in 13a and 13b. Decide who is going to say what.

d Make your presentation to the other students in your class.

Check your progress

1 Grammar

a Complete the sentences. Use the simple past form of the verbs.

Last night we ___watched___ (watch) a good show on TV. It [1]_____ (tell) the story of a famous man from India named Mahatma Gandhi. Gandhi [2]_____ (live) in South Africa when he was young, but in 1914 he [3]_____ (go) back to India. Gandhi [4]_____ (become) very famous there because he [5]_____ (think) fighting was bad. In 1947, the British [6]_____ (leave) India, but Gandhi [7]_____ (die) the next year. We [8]_____ (find) the show very interesting, and I [9]_____ (learn) a lot.

| | 9 |

b Complete the sentences. Use the simple past forms of the verbs.

1 We ___went___ (go) to the movies last week, but we ___didn't go___ (not go) shopping.

2 I _____ (write) six emails yesterday, but I _____ (not write) any letters.

3 Alan _____ (come) to the party, but Peter _____ (not come).

4 I _____ (eat) the fries, but I _____ (not eat) the carrots!

| | 6 |

c Write comparative sentences.

1 this test / difficult / the math test
   This test is more difficult than the math test.

2 Spanish / easy / Portuguese
   _____

3 my uncle's car / expensive / my father's
   _____
   _____

4 your homework / important / that computer game
   _____
   _____

5 her history teacher / good / my teacher
   _____
   _____

| | 4 |

2 Vocabulary

a Write the nouns in the box in the lists.

> ~~fun~~   work   an accident   the piano
> ~~tennis~~   bed   the movies   ice cream
> soccer   cards   ~~school~~   coffee

have

___fun___

_____

_____

_____

play

___tennis___

_____

_____

_____

go to

___school___

_____

_____

_____

| | 9 |

b Write the opposites of the adjectives.

1 boring   ___exciting___

2 dangerous   _____

3 old-fashioned _____

4 noisy   _____

| | 3 |

How did you do?

Check your score.

Total score	😊	😐	😞
31	Very good	OK	Not very good
Grammar	19 – 15	14 – 12	11 or less
Vocabulary	12 – 10	9 – 8	7 or less

Phonetic symbols

Consonants

Phonetic symbol:	Key words:
/p/	purple, apple
/b/	bicycle, hobby
/t/	table, litter
/d/	different, ride
/k/	desk, computer
/g/	game, dog
/f/	fun, sofa, photo
/v/	vegetables, favorite
/m/	mother, some
/n/	nose, lawn, know
/ŋ/	English, long
/s/	sit, pencil
/z/	zero, those
/w/	wind, one
/l/	laundry, small
/r/	red, rare
/y/	your, usually
/h/	house, who
/θ/	three, math
/ð/	father, this
/ʃ/	shop, station
/ʒ/	television, garage
/tʃ/	chocolate, kitchen
/dʒ/	jump, damage

Vowels

Phonetic symbol:	Key words:
/æ/	bad, taxi
/ɑ/	stop, opera
/ɛ/	chess, bed
/ə/	dramatic, the
/ɪ/	dish, sit
/i/	real, screen
/ʊ/	good, full
/u/	choose, view
/ʌ/	must, done
/ɔ/	strawberry, daughter

Vowels + /r/

Phonetic symbol:	Key words:
/ər/	first, shirt
/ɑr/	car
/ɔr/	horse
/ɛr/	their
/ʊr/	tourist
/ɪr/	ear

Diphthongs

Phonetic symbol:	Key words:
/eɪ/	play, train
/aɪ/	ice, night
/ɔɪ/	employer, noisy
/aʊ/	house, download
/oʊ/	no, window

Unit 1 Syllables

a ▶ CD1 T06 Listen and repeat the words in the table.

One syllable	Two syllables	Three syllables
bus	taxi	computer
phone	teacher	afternoon
desk	hotel	hamburger
-----------------	-----------------	-----------------
-----------------	-----------------	-----------------

b ▶ CD1 T07 Listen and write the words in the table.

Unit 2 Letter sounds

a Write the letters of the alphabet under the correct sounds.

/ɛ/	/eɪ/	/i/	/aɪ/
f	a	b	i

/oʊ/	/u/	/ɑr/
o	q	r

b ▶ CD1 T12 Listen, check and repeat.

Unit 3 from

a ▶ CD1 T25 Listen and repeat.

1 I'm from China.
2 Where are you from?
3 He's from Mexico.

b ▶ CD1 T25 Listen to 5a again. Is *from* the same in all of the sentences?

Unit 4 /ɪ/ and /i/

a ▶ CD1 T31 Listen to the two words.

big three

b Write the words from the box in the table.

> six   he   we   it   city
> cheap   video   fourteen

/ɪ/ big   /i/ three

....

....

....

....

c ▶ CD1 T32 Listen, check and repeat.

d ▶ CD1 T33 Listen and repeat as fast as you can.

He's in a video clip with six fit kids.

Unit 5 /s/, /z/ and /ɪz/

a ▶ CD1 T39 Listen and write the verbs in the lists.

> ~~goes~~   ~~watches~~   ~~stops~~   reads   likes
> studies   works   learns   gives   finishes

/s/	/z/	/ɪz/
stops	*goes*	*watches*
....	....	....
....	....	
	....	
	....	

b ▶ CD1 T39 Listen again and repeat.

Unit 6 /ð/ and /θ/

▶ CD1 T45 Listen and repeat.

/ð/		/θ/	
there	the	thousand	think
mother	father	thirty	three

Unit 7 /v/ have

a ▶ CD1 T51 Listen and repeat.

1	they've	4	I've	7	verb
2	we've	5	very	8	video
3	you've	6	five	9	volleyball

b Say the sentences.

1 We have five very long videos.
2 You have the wrong verb.
3 I have volleyball practice at seven.

c ▶ CD1 T52 Listen, check and repeat.

Unit 8 /w/ would

▶ CD1 T61 Listen and repeat.

1 Would you like a sandwich?
2 Are you the new waiter?
3 What do you want to eat?
4 Where in the world are you from?

Unit 9 Compound nouns

a ▶ CD2 T06 Listen. Is the stress on the first word or on the second word?

talk shows   game shows

sports programs   soap operas

b ▶ CD2 T06 Listen again and repeat.

Unit 10 Linking sounds

a ▶ CD2 T14 Listen to the four sentences. Can you hear the *t* in *don't*?

1 Don't laugh.
2 Don't cry.
3 Don't shout.
4 I don't like hamburgers.

b ▶ CD2 T15 Listen to these sentences. Can you hear the *t* in *don't*? Listen again and repeat.

1 Don't open the door.
2 Don't eat that.
3 I don't understand.
4 Don't ask me.

Unit 11 can/can't

a ▶ CD2 T23 Listen to the sentences. What's the difference between the sounds in *can* /ə/ and *can't* /æ/?

1 He can write on a computer, but he can't walk.
2 She can ride a bike, but she can't swim.
3 They can learn to count, but they can't learn to talk.
4 I can use a computer, but I can't draw pictures with it.

b ▶ CD2 T23 Listen again and repeat.

c ▶ **CD2 T24** Listen to the short conversations. Then listen again and repeat.

1 A: Can you swim?
   B: No, I can't.
2 A: Can you sing?
   B: Yes, but not very well!

Unit 12 /h/ *have*

▶ **CD2 T31** Listen and repeat the sentences.

1 Hi! Can I help you?
2 He can walk on his hands.
3 Are you hungry? Have a hamburger.
4 Henry and Hannah are having lunch in a hotel.

Unit 13 /æ/ and /ɛ/

a ▶ **CD2 T40** Listen and repeat the words.

/æ/	/ɛ/
black	yes
jacket	red
hamburger	dress
thanks	yellow
January	September

b Say the sentences.

1 I like the black jacket in the window.
2 I wear red in January and yellow in September.
3 She's wearing a black and red dress.

c ▶ **CD2 T41** Listen and repeat.

Unit 14 *was/wasn't* and *were/weren't*

a ▶ **CD2 T46** Listen and repeat the sentences.

1 He was only 22.
2 They were in Iowa.
3 It wasn't a warm night.
4 They weren't in New York.

b ▶ **CD2 T47** Listen and repeat the sentences.

1 A: Was he only 22?
   B: Yes, he was.
2 A: Were they in New York?
   B: No, they weren't.

c Work with a partner. Ask and answer the questions from Exercise 2d on page 93.

A: Were the three men in New York?
B: No, they weren't. They were in Iowa.

Unit 15 *-ed* endings

a ▶ **CD2 T55** Listen and repeat the sentences.

1 /t/ We watched a movie.
2 /d/ I lived in Chicago.
3 /ɪd/ He wanted ice cream.

b ▶ **CD2 T56** Listen and repeat the sentences.

1 I called a friend.
2 I called my friend.
3 He talked a lot.
4 He talked to the teacher.
5 We visited a friend.
6 We visited the museum.

c ▶ **CD2 T55 and T56** Listen to 3a and 3b again. Write these verbs in the table.

watch call want
live talk visit

/t/	/d/	/ɪd/
-----------------	-----------------	-----------------
-----------------	-----------------	-----------------

Unit 16 *than*

a ▶ **CD3 T03** Listen. How is *than* pronounced?

1 She's taller than me.
2 I'm older than him.
3 It's hotter than yesterday.
4 Our dog's bigger than yours.
5 This is more expensive than that one.

b ▶ **CD3 T03** Listen again and repeat.

Irregular verbs

Base form	Simple past	Base form	Simple past
be	was/were	let	let
become	became	lose	lost
begin	began	make	made
break	broke	meet	met
bring	brought	pay	paid
buy	bought	put	put
can	could	read	read
catch	caught	ride	rode
choose	chose	run	ran
come	came	say	said
cut	cut	see	saw
do	did	sell	sold
drink	drank	send	sent
drive	drove	sing	sang
eat	ate	sit	sat
fall	fell	sleep	slept
feel	felt	speak	spoke
find	found	spend	spent
fly	flew	swim	swam
forget	forgot	take	took
get	got	teach	taught
give	gave	tell	told
go	went	think	thought
have	had	understand	understood
hear	heard	wake up	woke up
hit	hit	wear	wore
hurt	hurt	win	won
know	knew	write	wrote
leave	left		

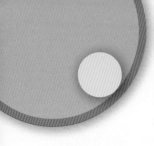

Project 1

A poster presentation about a band or singer

1 Research

a Work in groups of three or four. Choose a singer or a band your group likes. Collect information about the singer or the band. Use these questions to help you:

- What's the singer's or band's name?
- Where is he/she from? Where are they from?
- How old are they?
- What instruments do they play?
- What are your favorite songs or albums?

b Write a short text about the singer or band. Use the example and the questions in Exercise 1a to help you.

c Collect pictures. Get a large piece of paper or cardboard for your poster. Put the pictures on the paper and add your texts.

d Get a song by the singer or band that you like.

2 Prepare the presentation

a Practice presenting your poster. Read your text aloud.

3 Presentation

a Present your poster to another group or the class. At the end of your presentation, play a song by the singer or band.

COBRA STARSHIP

Cobra Starship is an American band. There are five people in the band: Gabe Saporta (who is the band leader), Ryland Blackinton, Alex Suarez, Nate Novarro and Victoria Asher.

Gabe Saporta is from New York, and he's the lead singer. Ryland Blackinton is from Massachusetts, and he is on lead guitar and the synthesizer. Alex Suarez is on bass guitar, and Nate Novarro is on the drums. Victoria Asher is American, but some of her family is from Britain. They are all 25–30 years old.

Cobra Starship has three albums – *While the City Sleeps, We Rule the Streets* (2006), *Viva la Cobra* (2007) and *Hot Mess* (2009).

We think their music is fantastic! Our favorite songs are "Snakes on a Plane" and "The City Is at War" – great songs! Check out their music. We're sure you'll like Cobra Starship!

Project 2
A tourist brochure

1 Research

a Work in groups of three or four. Choose a town or city. Find some facts about the town or city and write notes. Use these questions and the example to help you:

- What kinds of stores are there in the town/city?
- What interesting places are there for tourists? (For example, museums, markets, cafés/restaurants.)
- Are there any interesting places near the town/city?
- Why is the town/city special?

b Collect photos or draw pictures of your town/city.

2 Make the leaflet

a Get a large piece of paper. Your teacher will show you how to fold it.

b Write your information. Use these ideas and the example to help you:

- On the front cover page, write *Come and visit* and add the name of the town or city. Add a picture of an interesting place in your town/city.
- On pages 1 and 2, draw a map of the town/city or a part of it. Write the names of the places and streets.
- On pages 3–6, add pictures of places in the town/city and write your information.

c If you have time, write a quiz about the town/city.

Izmir is a famous and important city in the west of Turkey.

It is near the ocean, and it's very beautiful. There are a lot of things to do and see in Izmir! Try these.

Visit the famous, 100-year-old Clock Tower. Walk around the Agora, a very old market from the time when Izmir was called Smyrna.

Do you like shopping? Kemeralti is a great market. You can buy a lot of Turkish crafts to take home with you, and you can also buy food, like fish. The fish in Turkey is fantastic!

At the end of the day, walk along the boardwalk by the ocean where there are many cafés. You can sit and have a snack and watch the sunset. It's beautiful!

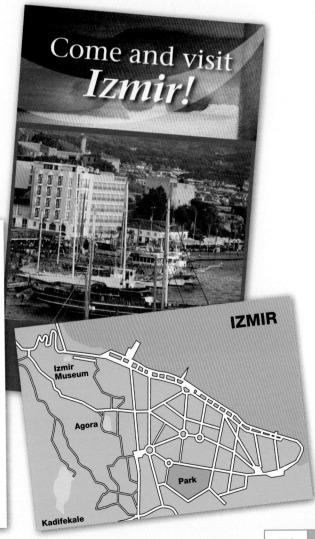

Come and visit *Izmir!*

IZMIR

Izmir Museum

Agora

Park

Kadifekale

Project 3

A class survey

1 Prepare the survey

a Work in groups of three or four. Choose one topic about free time. Use these ideas to help you:

- music
- TV
- sports
- shopping

b Together, write four or five questions to ask other students in the class. Use the example to help you.

Sports

Name Barbara

1 What kinds of sports do you like?   .Tennis. and. soccer..

2 How often do you play sports?   ....

3 Who's your favorite athlete?   ....

4 Do you like watching sports on TV?   ....

5 Do you .... ?   ....

c Each student in your group asks two or three students from another group and takes notes.

2 Write the report

a Work with your group. Tell the other students your information. Write the results on one piece of paper.

> Barbara likes tennis and soccer. She doesn't play soccer, but she watches it on TV. Her favorite athlete is ...

b In your group, write a report and present your work to the class.

> Three people in our class play soccer after school (two boys and one girl).
> All the boys in our survey like watching sports on TV, but only three girls like watching sports on TV ...

Project 4

A presentation on changes in your country

1 Research

a Work in groups of three or four. In your group, choose one or two topics you would like to focus on. Look at these ideas to help you:

- town/city life (shopping, streets, buildings, roads and transportation)
- school life
- free time activities (sports, movies, plays, TV, etc.)
- food and eating out
- family and home life

b What do you want to find out about the past? How are things different now? Write some questions to help you get information. Look at these example questions:

Family and home life

- Were families bigger or smaller in your country 50 years ago?
- Did young people get married and leave home later or earlier than they do now?
- Did older people, like grandparents, usually live with their families?
- Were houses smaller than they are now? Did children share their bedrooms?

c Talk to older people you know, who are from your country, for example, your grandparents. Ask them how things were 50 years ago and how things are different now. Write down their answers, or record them.

d Find more information about your country as it was 50 years ago. Look on the Internet or in a library or museum. Try to get some photos of your country from 50 years ago.

2 Presentation

a In your group, organize your information. You can present your information on a large piece of paper or cardboard. Write your information and add any photos you have.

b Take turns to presenting your information. If you can, use photographs to illustrate your presentation. First, tell the class what your presentation is about.

This presentation is about family and home life in our country 50 years ago, compared to today. In the 1960s, families in ... were ... than today ...

Notes

NOTES

Thanks and acknowledgments

The authors would like to thank a number of people whose support has proved invaluable during the planning, writing and production process of *American English in Mind*.

First of all we would like to thank the numerous teachers and students in many countries of the world who have used the first edition of English in Mind. Their enthusiasm for the course, and the detailed feedback and valuable suggestions we got from many of them were an important source of inspiration and guidance for us in developing the concept and in the creation of *American English in Mind*.

In particular, the authors and publishers would like to thank the following teachers who gave up their valuable time for classroom observations, interviews and focus groups:

Brazil
Warren Cragg (ASAP Idiomas); Angela Pinheiro da Cruz (Colégio São Bento; Carpe Diem); Ana Paula Vedovato Maestrello (Colégio Beatíssima Virgem Maria); Natália Mantovanelli Fontana (Lord's Idiomas); Renata Condi de Souza (Colégio Rio Branco, Higienópolis Branch); Alexandra Arruda Cardoso de Almeida (Colégio Guilherme Dumont Villares / Colégio Emilie de Villeneuve); Gisele Siqueira (Speak Up); Ana Karina Giusti Mantovani (Idéia Escolas de Línguas); Maria Virgínia G. B. de Lebron (UFTM / private lessons); Marina Piccinato (Speak Up); Patrícia Nero (Cultura Inglesa / Vila Mariana); Graziela Barroso (Associação Alumni); Francisco Carlos Peinado (Wording); Maria Lúcia Sciamarelli (Colégio Divina Providencia / Jundiaí); Deborah Hallal Jorge (Nice Time Language Center); Lilian Itzicovitch Leventhal (Colégio I. L. Peretz); Dulcinéia Ferreira (One Way Línguas); and Priscila Prieto and Carolina Cruz Marques (Seven Idiomas).

Colombia
Luz Amparo Chacón (Gimnasio Los Monjes); Mayra Barrera; Diana de la Pava (Colegio de la Presentación Las Ferias); Edgar Ardila (Col. Mayor José Celestino Mutis); Sandra Cavanzo B. (Liceo Campo David); Claudia Susana Contreras and Luz Marína Zuluaga (Colegio Anglo Americano); Celina Roldán and Angel Torres (Liceo Cervantes del Norte); Nelson Navarro; Maritza Ruiz Martín; Francisco Mejía, and Adriana Villalba (Colegio Calasanz).

Ecuador
Paul Viteri (Colegio Andino, Quito); William E. Yugsan (Golden Gate Academy – Quito); Irene Costales (Unidad Educativa Cardinal Spellman Femenino); Vinicio Sanchez and Sandra Milena Rodríguez (Colegio Santo Domingo de Guzmán); Sandra Rigazio and María Elena Moncayo (Unidad Educativa Tomás Moro, Quito); Jenny Alexandra Jara Recalde and Estanislao Javier Pauta (COTAC, Quito); Verónica Landázuri and Marisela Madrid (Unidad Educativa "San Francisco de Sales"); Oswaldo Gonzalez and Monica Tamayo (Angel Polibio Chaves School, Quito); Rosario Llerena and Tania Abad (Isaac Newton, Quito); María Fernanda Mármol Mazzini and Luis Armijos (Unidad Educativa Letort, Quito); and Diego Bastidas and Gonzalo Estrella (Colegio Gonzaga, Quito).

Mexico
Connie Alvarez (Colegio Makarenko); Julieta Zelinski (Colegio Williams); Patricia Avila (Liceo Ibero Mexicano); Patricia Cervantes de Brofft (Colegio Frances del Pedregal); Alicia Sotelo (Colegio Simon Bolivar); Patricia Lopez (Instituto Mexico, A.C.); Maria Eugenia Fernandez Castro (Instituto Oriente Arboledas); Lilian Ariadne Lozano Bustos (Universidad Tecmilenio); Maria del Consuelo Contreras Estrada (Liceo Albert Einstein); Alfonso Rene Pelayo Garcia (Colegio Tomas Alva Edison); Ana Pilar Gonzalez (Instituto Felix de Jesus Rougier); and Blanca Kreutter (Instituto Simon Bolivar).

Our heartfelt thanks go to the *American English in Mind* team for their cooperative spirit, their many excellent suggestions and their dedication, which have been characteristic of the entire editorial process: Paul Phillips, Amy E. Hawley, Kelley Perrella, Eric Zuarino, Pam Harris, Kate Powers, Brigit Dermott, Kate Spencer, Heather McCarron, Keaton Babb, Roderick Gammon, Hugo Loyola, Howard Siegelman, Colleen Schumacher, Margaret Brooks, Kathryn O'Dell, Genevieve Kocienda, Lisa Hutchins, and Lynne Robertson.

We would also like to thank the teams of educational consultants, representatives and managers working for Cambridge University Press in various countries around the world. Space does not allow us to mention them all by name here, but we are extremely grateful for their support and their commitment.

Thanks to the team at Pentacor for giving the book its design; the staff at Full House Productions for the audio recordings; and Lightning Pictures for the video.

Last but not least, we would like to thank our partners, Mares and Adriana, for their support.

The authors and publishers acknowledge the following sources of copyright material and are grateful for the permissions granted. While every effort has been made, it has not always been possible to identify the sources of all the material used, or to trace all copyright holders. If any omissions are brought to our notice, we will be happy to include the appropriate acknowledgements on reprinting.

Are We Alone on p.25. Words and music by Steve Hall. Copyright © Bell Voice Recordings, licensed to Cambridge University Press. Bell Voice recordings for the recording.
Don't Stop on p.67. Words & Music by Christine McVie © Copyright 1976 Fleetwood Mac Music, USA. Universal Music Publishing MGB Limited and Universal Music – Careers. Copyright renewed. All Rights Reserved. International Copyright Secured. Used by permission of Music Sales Limited and Hal Leonard Corporation. Bell Voice Recordings for the sound-a-like recording by Fleetwood Mac.

The publishers are grateful to the following illustrators: Graham Kennedy, Tracey Knight (Lemonade), Rob McClurkan, Red Jelly Illustration, David Semple, Mark Watkinson (Illustration)

The publishers are grateful to the following for permission to reproduce photographic material:
Key: l = left, c = center, r = right, t = top, b = bottom, u = upper, lo = lower, f = far
akg-images p94(c); Alamy pp 4(9), 4(13), 23(bc), 23(b), 30(b), 44(r), 46(b), 48 (c), 56, 58(c), 62(br), 70, 78, 78(br), 78(t),80(A), 80(B), 80(C), 80(F), 84, 86(t), 87(A), 87(C), 87(D), 90(t), 95, 97(cl), 97(cr), 100(c), 105(l), 106(bl), 106(br), 106(cl), 106(tl), 102(tr), 108(b), 108(tl), 108(tr), 119(r), 120(bl), 120(t); Corbis UK Ltd. pp16(bc), 30 (c), 62(t), 80(D), 80(E), 90(br), 90(cr), 100(b), 102(r), 105(br), 106(bc), 120(br), 121(b); Frank Lane Picture Agencypp44(l), 49(b), 49(t), Getty Images48(tl), 92(b), 92(cl), 92(cr), 94(t), 97(tr), 121(c), 121(t); Image State p44(bl); iStockphoto pp 48(tc), 48(tr), 86(bl), 86(br), 106(c); Mary Evans Picture Library p106(tc); NASA p102(l); Nokia p4(14); Patrick McGuire p58(b); Photolibrary Grouppp18(1), 18(4), 75, 86(c), 119(l); Press Associationimages pp10(bc), 20(bl), 25(br), 25(cr), 28, 30(cl), 46(t), 46(tc), 92(t); Rex Features pp 16(bl), 16(br), 16(t), 17(1), 17(2), 17(3), 17(4), 20(br), 20(tl), 20(tr), 23(t), 23(tc), 25(bc), 25(bl), 25(c), 25(cl), 25(tr), 30(cr), 46(bc), 94(b), 100(t), 102(c), 105(tr), 118(b), 118(t); ScottishViewpoint p90(bl); Shutterstock pp 4(1), 4(8), 4(10), 4(11), 4(15), 4(16), 4(2), 4(13), 4(4), 4(6), 18(3), 21, 49(tc), 63(r), 87(B), 97(tl); www.teamhoyt.com pp72(b), 72(t); Zooid Pictures p70.
Alamy/©Kim Karpeles p 4 (cl), Cutcaster/©Claude Beaubien p 4 (cr), iStockphoto /©Sharon Dominick p 4 (cr), Veer/Getty Images/©Somos p 7 (tl), iStockphoto/©FreezeFrameStudio p 7 (tr), Shutterstock /©Michael C. Gray p 6 (cl), age fotostock/©Comstock Images p 6 (cr), Getty Images/©OJO Images/Chris Ryan p 7 (cl), Getty Images/©Jose Luis Pelaez Inc/Blend Images p 7 (c), Getty Images/©Jupiterimages/Workbook Stock p 7 (cr), Cutcaster/©Mariusz Jurgielewicz p 18 (tr), iStockphoto /©sculpies p 20 (br), Getty Images/©Jon Kopaloff/FilmMagic p 20 (tr), Getty Images/©Matthew Peyton p 20 (cr), Getty Images/©EMMANUEL DUNAND/AFP p 20 (cl), Getty Images ©Tony Barson/WireImage p 23 (br), iStockphoto/©Daniel Norman p 23 (bl), Getty Images/©Ethan Miller p 25 (tc),Getty Images/©Alex Wong p 30 (cr), Shutterstock/©Monkey Business Images p 34 (tc), Corbis/©Nicole Hill/Rubberball p 34 (bl), Getty Images/David Malan/Gallo Images p 35 (cl), Getty Images/©Reggie Casagrande/Workbook Stock p 35 (c), iStockphoto/Justin Horrocks p 35 (cr), iStockphoto/©Konstantin Sutyagin p 35 (bl), Getty Images/©Mark Edward Atkinson/Blend Images p 35 (bc), Getty Images/©Ronnie Kaufman/Larry Hirshowitz/Blend Images p 35 (br), Alamy/©Michael Dwyer p 37 (tl), Alamy/©Krista Rossow p 36 (tc), Alamy ©Michael Dwyer p 37 (bl), Getty Images ©Michael Ivins/Boston Red Sox/ MLB Photos p 36 (br),Alamy/©Mike Perry p 37 (cl), Alamy ©Anonymous Donor p 36 (bc), Shutterstock ©Oleg Mit p 42 (c), ©iStockphoto p 48 (hamster), iStockphoto/©Eric Isselée p 48 (rabbit), iStockphoto/©Sirko Hartmann p 48 (sleddog), iStockphoto ©ShyMan p 50 (tr), Getty Images/©Tim Graham p 50 (bl) ©Myrleen Pearson p 50 (c), Getty Images/©Teubner/StockFood Creative p 50 (br), Getty Images/©Paul Avis/Photodisc p 58 (cr), Getty Images/©Photo by David Hume Kennerly p 60 (cr), Getty Images/©Photo by Monty Brinton/CBS p60 (bl), Getty Images ©Photo by Valerie Macon p 60 (r), iStockphoto/©Galina Barskaya p 63 (tl), AP Images/©Photo by: NBCU Photo Bank p 62(bl), Getty Images/©Nathaniel S. Butler/NBAE p 63(br), Alamy ©Images-USA p 76(A), Shutterstock/©muzsy p 76(B),Shutterstock/©Bruce Yeung p 76 (C), Getty Images ©GLYN KIRK/AFP p 76 (D), Shutterstock/©KennStilger47 p 76 (E), iStockphoto/©dswebb p 76 (F), iStockphoto/©Keith Binns p 76 (cl), iStockphoto/©Kevin Russ p 76 (bl), Getty Images/©Wesley Hitt/Photodisc p 77 (br), Getty Images/©Jeff J Mitchell p 90 (cr), Getty Images/© David Murray and Jules Selmes/Dorling Kindersley p 91 (tr), AP Photo/©Dave Martin p 91 (cr), Getty Images/©Photo by Chris Graythen p 91 (bl), Shutterstock/©ArielMartin p 98 (tr), Getty Images/©Photo by CBS Photo Archive p 104 (tr), Getty Images/©Photo by George Karger/Pix Inc./Time Life Pictures p 104 (br), Getty Images/©Photo by CBS Photo Archive p 104 (bl), iStockphoto/© technotr p 111 (br), Getty Images/©Andreas Feininger/Time Life Pictures p 112 (c), Shutterstock/©gary718 p 112 (b),

The publishers are grateful to the following for their assistance with commissioned photographs:
Alex Medeville

DVD-ROM Instructions

American English in Mind can be run directly from the DVD-ROM and does not require installation. However, you can also install *American English in Mind* and run it from your hard drive. This will make the DVD-ROM run more quickly.

Start the DVD-ROM

Windows PC
- Insert the *American English in Mind* DVD-ROM into your DVD-ROM drive.
- If Autorun is enabled, the DVD-ROM will start automatically.
- If Autorun is not enabled, open **My Computer** and then **D:** (where D is the letter of your DVD-ROM drive). Then double click on the *American English in Mind* icon.

Mac OS X
- Insert the *American English in Mind* DVD-ROM into your DVD-ROM drive.
- Double-click on the DVD-ROM icon on your desktop to open it.
- Double-click on the *American English in Mind* Mac OS X icon.

Install the DVD-ROM to your hard drive (recommended)

Windows PC
- Go to **My Computer** and then **D:** (where D is the letter of your DVD-ROM drive).
- Right-click on *Explore*.
- Double-click on *Install American English in Mind to hard drive*.
- Follow the installation instructions on your screen.

Mac OS X
- Double-click on the DVD-ROM icon on your desktop to open it.
- Create a folder on your computer.
- Copy the content of the DVD-ROM into this folder.
- Double-click on the *American English in Mind* Mac OS X icon.

Listen and practice on your CD player
You can listen to and practice language from the Student's Book Pronunciation, Culture in Mind and Photostory activities. You can also listen to and practice the Workbook Pronunciation and Listening activities.

What's on the DVD-ROM?

- **Interactive practice activities**
  Extra practice of Grammar, Vocabulary, English Pronunciation, Reading and Writing. Click on a set of unit numbers (1–2 through 15–16) at the top of the screen. Then choose an activity and click on it to start.

- **Word list**
  Pronunciation and definitions. Click on *Word list* on the left side of the screen. Then choose a word to hear its pronunciation. You can also add your own notes.

- **Self-test**
  Click on *Self-test*, and choose a set of unit numbers (1–2 through 15–16) on the left side of the screen. You can also test yourself on multiple sets of units.

- **Game**
  This is extra practice of Grammar and Vocabulary. Click on the game controller icon at the top of the screen. Click on a set of unit numbers (1–2 through 15–16), and choose a character. Click on start to begin the game. You can also choose all the units.

System Requirements
- 512MB of RAM (1GB recommended for video)
- 1GB free hard disk space (if installing to hard disk)
- 800 x 600 resolution or higher
- speakers or headphones
- a microphone if you wish to record yourself speaking

For PC
- Windows XP, Vista or 7

For Mac
- Mac OSX 10.4 or 10.5
- 1.2 GHz G4 processor or higher

Support

If you experience difficulties with this DVD-ROM, please visit:

http://www.cambridge.org/elt/multimedia/help